DIGITAL PHOTOGRAPHY
QuickSteps
Second Edition

DIGITAL PHOTOGRAPHY
QuickSteps
Second Edition

DOUG SAHLIN

New York Chicago San Francisco
Lisbon London Madrid Mexico City
Milan New Delhi San Juan
Seoul Singapore Sydney Toronto

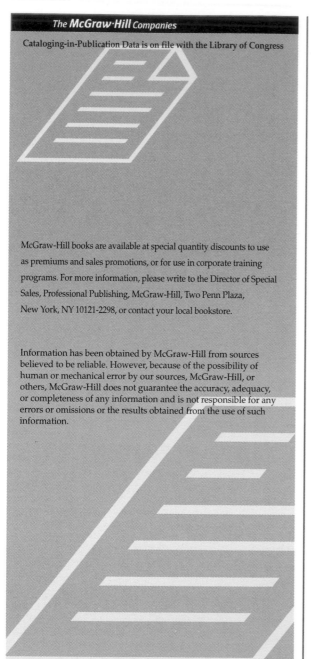

The McGraw·Hill Companies

Cataloging-in-Publication Data is on file with the Library of Congress

McGraw-Hill books are available at special quantity discounts to use as premiums and sales promotions, or for use in corporate training programs. For more information, please write to the Director of Special Sales, Professional Publishing, McGraw-Hill, Two Penn Plaza, New York, NY 10121-2298, or contact your local bookstore.

Information has been obtained by McGraw-Hill from sources believed to be reliable. However, because of the possibility of human or mechanical error by our sources, McGraw-Hill, or others, McGraw-Hill does not guarantee the accuracy, adequacy, or completeness of any information and is not responsible for any errors or omissions or the results obtained from the use of such information.

DIGITAL PHOTOGRAPHY QUICKSTEPS, SECOND EDITION

1234567890 CCI CCI 01987

ISBN-13:   978-0-07-148298-1
ISBN-10:   0-07-148298-9

SPONSORING EDITOR / Roger Stewart

EDITORIAL SUPERVISOR / Janet Walden

PROJECT MANAGER / Samik Roy Chowdhury (International Typesetting and Composition)

ACQUISITIONS COORDINATOR / Carly Stapleton

SERIES CREATORS AND EDITORS / Marty and Carole Matthews

TECHNICAL EDITOR / Dave Huss

COPY EDITOR / Lisa McCoy

PROOFREADER / Francesca Ferrie

INDEXER / Claire Splan

PRODUCTION SUPERVISOR / Jean Bodeaux

COMPOSITION / International Typesetting and Composition

ILLUSTRATION / International Typesetting and Composition

ART DIRECTOR, COVER / Jeff Weeks

COVER DESIGN / Pattie Lee

SERIES DESIGN / Bailey Cunningham

Dedicated to the memory of my best friend and mentor,
my mother Inez. Wish you were here to see this, kiddo.

About the Author

Doug Sahlin is an author, photographer, and instructor living in Lakeland, Florida. He has written 18 books on digital photography and computer applications, including the popular *How to Do Everything with Adobe Acrobat 8.0*. In addition, he has written and co-written books on video-editing and image-editing applications. Doug is also president of Superb Images, Inc., a wedding and event photography company. His clients include actors, authors, fashion models, and business professionals. His work has been seen in print and on the Web.

Contents at a Glance

Contents

1

2

Chapter 3 Shooting Like a Pro 41

Preface

Welcome to the second edition of *Digital Photography QuickSteps*. That's right, the second edition. The whole landscape of digital photography has changed since the first edition of this book was published in 2004. Digital cameras with seven-megapixel resolution that can fit in your shirt pocket are now a reality. Memory cards have increased in capacity, shutter lag is almost nonexistent, and camera film is almost a thing of the past. In this book you'll find the latest information for choosing a digital camera that suits your needs. You'll also find information that will help you become a better photographer. You'll learn which camera settings you should use for taking a snapshot of your Aunt Mollie, which settings you should use to photograph Danica Patrick driving the Indy 500, and which settings you should use to photograph landscapes, wildlife, stuff you want to sell on eBay, and so on. You'll also learn tips on how to conserve camera battery life and maximize memory card usage, as well as how to accessorize your camera. In the second half of the book, you'll learn how to get the images into your computer and edit them with Photoshop Elements. This part of the book also shows you how to add pizzazz to your images with special effects, how to turn your images into slide shows, Web galleries, and much more. I hope you enjoy the book and get a lot out of it. Happy shooting.

–Doug Sahlin

Acknowledgments

Even though a single name appears on the cover of this book, the project would not be possible without a cast of many fine folks. Many thanks to Roger Stewart for making this project possible. Thanks to Carly Stapleton for making sure the chapters and accompanying illustrations were delivered to the right folks at the right time. Thanks to Lisa McCoy, copyeditor, and to Sam, project manager at ITC, for taking this bull by the horns (that would be me, the author, a card-carrying Taurus) and making sure that the words you read are squeaky clean. Thanks to Dave Huss, technical editor and fellow shutterbug. Thanks to Margot Maley Hutchison for handling the fine print.

Thanks to fellow authors Bonnie Blake, Joyce Evans, and Ken Milburn for being sources of inspiration, good friends, and ecologically sane citizens of this planet. Special thanks to my friends, mentors, and family members, especially you, Karen and Ted. Special kudos to my social secretary, Niki the Cat, whom I'm currently training to make origami from the many credit card offers I receive.

Introduction

QuickSteps books are recipe books for computer users. They answer the question, "How do I...?" by providing quick sets of steps to accomplish the most common tasks in a particular program or technology, such as digital photography. The sets of steps are the central focus of the book. QuickFacts sidebars give you pertinent information associated with the chapter text, while QuickSteps sidebars show you how to quickly do many small functions or tasks that support the primary functions. Notes, Tips, and Cautions augment the steps, but are presented in such a manner as not to interrupt the flow of the steps. The brief introductions are minimal rather than narrative, and numerous illustrations and figures, many with callouts, support the steps. QuickSteps books are organized by function and the tasks needed to perform that function. Each function is a chapter. Each task, or "How To," contains the steps needed for accomplishing the function, along with relevant Notes, Tips, Cautions, and screenshots. Tasks will be easy to find through the following:

- The Table of Contents, which lists the functional areas (chapters) and tasks in the order they are presented.

- A How To list of tasks on the opening page of each chapter. The index, with its alphabetical list of terms used in describing the functions and tasks, makes it easy for you to find specific information within the book.

- Color-coded tabs for each chapter or functional area, with an index to the tabs just before the Table of Contents.

Conventions Used
in This Book

Digital Photography QuickSteps uses several conventions designed to make the book easier for you to follow. Among these are:

- A ✎ in the Table of Contents or the How To list in each chapter references a QuickFacts sidebar in a chapter.

- A 💬 in the Table of Contents or the How To list in each chapter references a QuickSteps sidebar in a chapter.

- **Bold** type is used for words on the screen that you are to do something with, such as click **Save As** or **Open**.

- *Italic* type is used for a word or phrase that is being defined or otherwise deserves special emphasis.

- <u>Underlined</u> type is used for text that you are to type from the keyboard. SMALL CAPITAL LETTERS are used for keys on the keyboard, such as **ENTER** and **SHIFT**.

- When you are expected to enter a command, you are told to press the key(s). If you are to enter text or numbers, you are told to type them. Specific letters or numbers to be typed will be underlined.

- When you need to perform a menu command, you will be told, "Click File | Open."

How to...

Chapter 1

Stepping into Digital Photography

Choosing your digital camera is your first step into the wonderful world of digital photography. Whether you're a casual photographer or a seasoned veteran, you'll need a digital camera with features that suit your needs. This chapter will help you get started.

Understand Digital Photography

Before you buy a digital camera, you should know a little about a digital camera's main components and features, as well as some of the terms associated with digital photography. This knowledge will enable you to make a good decision when choosing your first digital camera, or when upgrading to a more sophisticated digital camera as your interest in photography grows. It will also prevent you from buying an expensive camera with more bells and whistles than you need.

QUICK**FACTS**

UNDERSTANDING IMAGE SENSORS

CCD (charge coupled device) and CMOS
(complementary metal oxide semiconductor) devices
have rows and columns of sensors called photosites.
Each photosite records a portion of the image. When
the shutter opens, each photosite collects and stores
photons. After the picture is taken, the photosite
information is converted, row by row, from analog to
digital and then transferred to the camera storage device.

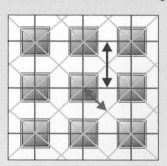

Frequently Asked Questions about Digital Photography

Digital technology opens up all sorts of wonderful possibilities for the world
of photography. The latest and greatest technology, however, often creates
more questions for the user than it answers. The following list of commonly
asked questions and answers will provide you with a basic overview of digital
camera technology. Later in the book, as we get into more detailed discussions
of camera features and image editing you will be able to refer back to these
questions if you need to.

Q: How does a digital camera work?

A: A digital camera has a lens and shutter, just like a film camera. Both types
of cameras use a metering device to determine the proper exposure needed
to record the image. A conventional camera records the image on film, which
needs to be processed in a lab before you see the results. The digital camera's
image sensor acts as the film, recording the information in digital format,
after which the image is transferred to the camera's storage device. With the
exception of the RAW format, the picture is processed in the camera, and you
see the results almost immediately on the camera's LCD monitor. If you shoot
using your camera's RAW format, the LCD monitor displays an image of what
the camera recorded.

Q: What is an image sensor?

A: The image sensor records images by converting light signals to electrical
signals, which is then processed by your camera and stored in digital form.
Digital cameras use two kinds of image sensors: CCD (charge coupled device)
or CMOS (complementary metal oxide semiconductor). CMOS sensors are
thinner and can accommodate additional circuitry for features such as image
stabilization and dust removal. They also consume less battery power than
CCDs. High-tech cameras with CMOS sensors feature built-in noise reduction
circuitry, which assures you of sharper pictures in most conditions. Most digital
SLR (single lens reflex) cameras use CMOS sensors, although there are a few
notable exceptions that use CCD sensors.

Figure 1-1: Memory cards come in a variety of capacities, shapes, and sizes.

Q: How do digital cameras store images?

A: Modern digital cameras use removable storage media, as shown in Figure 1-1. Think of camera storage devices as your digital film. They serve the same function as the hard drive on your computer, but without as many moving parts. Storage device capacity is measured in megabytes (MB) or, for ultra-high capacity cards, gigabytes (GB)—the same units of measure used to measure computer hard drive capacity. The number of images you can store on a memory card is determined by image resolution, which we will discuss later. The following storage devices are commonly used by digital cameras:

● **CompactFlash** cards are used on older consumer point-and-shoot cameras, as well as on high-end digital cameras and professional digital SLR cameras. They are sturdy and have storage capacities ranging from 8 MB to 16 GB

● **Secure Digital** (SD) cards are smaller than CompactFlash cards and yet are relatively sturdy. They are used for information storage on many devices, including PDA (personal digital assistant) devices and digital cameras. Secure Digital cards are available with capacities as high as 4 GB. Owners of MMC (Multimedia Card) cards may be able to use the cards in their digital cameras, as they are the same physical size as SD cards.

● **Microdrives** are miniature hard drives and will fit all cameras that accept CompactFlash II cards. They are less expensive than CompactFlash cards of the same capacity and can store up to 8 GB of data.

● **Memory Stick** is the storage media used by Sony digital cameras. Sony's Memory Stick cards have capacities as high as 4 GB.

● **Memory Stick Duo** is another storage media used by Sony digital cameras. In order to accommodate the smaller cameras on the market, this memory card is smaller than the standard Memory Stick. In fact, it's smaller than the miniscule SD card. Memory Stick Duo is available with a capacity as high as 4 GB.

● **SmartMedia** cards were used by certain older Olympus models. New-model Olympus cameras use the xD-Picture cards. SmartMedia cards are still available for older-model Olympus cameras, with a capacity as high as 128 MB.

● **xD-Picture** cards are used by Fujifilm and Olympus digital cameras, and are available with a capacity as high as 2 GB. The original xD cards were available in capacities ranging from 16 MB to 512 MB. Newer xD cards are designated as Type H, with capacities from 256 MB to 1 GB, and Type M, with capacities from 256 MB to 2 GB. If you're purchasing Type H or Type M cards for older cameras, make sure they are compatible.

Figure 1-2: A high-resolution image is comprised of millions of pixels.

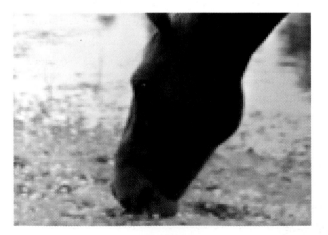

Figure 1-3: Individual pixels are squares of solid color.

Q: What is a pixel?

A: Short for "picture element," a pixel is a single point of color in a digital display. A pixel is composed of varying degrees of three colors: red, green, and blue (or RGB). The blending of varying amounts of RGB gives each pixel its distinctive color. On a true-color (24-bit) monitor, millions of pixels are arranged in rows and columns packed so tightly together that they appear to blend into continuous tones and create a solid image. The image size in pixels refers to the number of vertical and horizontal rows of pixels that make up the image. Figure 1-2 shows a high-resolution image. Figure 1-3 is a magnified section of the image, which allows you to see the pixels that comprise it.

Q: What is image resolution and how does it relate to image size?

A: Image resolution is the number of pixels per inch used to create an image. When you work with an image that has a high resolution, you can readily see the difference in quality, because the additional pixels make it possible to reproduce subtle variations in color. An image that measures 10 × 8 inches at a resolution of 300 pixels per inch (ppi) has pixel dimensions of 3000 × 2400. If you lower the resolution while keeping the pixel dimensions constant, you can print a larger image. However, the image will not be as sharp as the original was at a higher resolution. For example, if you change the resolution of an image with pixel dimensions of 3000 × 2400 from 300 ppi to 200 ppi, the resulting print measures 15 × 12 inches. The 200 ppi image will not be as sharp as the 300 ppi image because the pixels are larger.

UNDERSTANDING IMAGE QUALITY

A 10 × 8-inch image at 72 ppi has pixel dimensions of 720 × 576. Images for computer viewing require a resolution of only 72 ppi. Photo-quality printed images, however, require a resolution of at least 200 ppi or, preferably, 300 ppi. If you print a 10 × 8-inch image with pixel dimensions of 720 × 576 (a resolution of 72 ppi), the result will be blocky and unsatisfactory. If, on the other hand, you print an image with pixel dimensions of 3000 × 2400 at 300 ppi, you will get a photo-realistic 10 × 8-inch image, with a smooth blending of color. Most digital cameras have a native resolution of 180 ppi or better.

Compact digital cameras have smaller sensors than their larger brethren. Therefore, information is recorded on smaller photosites. Some compact digital cameras with resolutions of 5 megapixels and up may have visible noise in images shot at ISO ratings of 400 and above.

Increasing the ISO setting can introduce digital noise, which is similar to the graininess that appears in images recorded with film cameras using high-speed film. Many cameras have noise filters built-in. You can also purchase third-party noise filters as plug-ins for your image-editing application.

Q: What are megapixels?

A: A megapixel, the unit of measure for the number of pixels captured by a digital camera image sensor, is a million pixels. For example, an 8.0-megapixel camera is capable of creating images with a maximum image size of 3456 × 2304 pixels (a total of 7,962,264 pixels). The maximum image size of your camera determines the maximum size image you can print. To determine the maximum print size of the 8.0-megapixel camera, divide the number of pixels by the image resolution. For example, if the camera has an image resolution of 240 ppi, and you shoot a picture with an image size of 3456 × 2304 pixels, you can print a photo-quality image that is 14.4 × 9.6 inches. It's important to note that higher-resolution images are larger in file size, which means you can store fewer of them on your camera's removable storage media.

Q: What is an ISO rating?

A: ISO (International Organization for Standardization) refers to the sensitivity of your digital camera. This rating is similar to the speed of camera film. Film speed cannot be changed, whereas most digital and all digital SLR cameras enable you to change ISO ratings as needed. When you shoot in normal lighting conditions, a low ISO setting will give you the best results. When shooting in low-light conditions, choosing a higher ISO setting makes the camera more sensitive, enabling you to capture images in such settings without using a tripod. The ratings range from ISO 50 (low sensitivity with fine image detail) to ISO 3200 (high sensitivity, which may contain considerable noise). There are even a few cameras with ISO 6400 on the market. However, these cameras produce a lot of digital noise and the images are almost unusable.

Q: What are image file formats?

A: When your digital camera processes an image, it takes the data from the image sensor and processes it into the format you specify. The file format you specify, combined with the image size, determines the file size and, therefore, the amount of room needed on your camera's memory card. Most digital cameras use the JPEG (Joint Photographic Experts Group) file format, while some use the TIFF (Tagged Information File Format) and RAW file format.

QUICKFACTS

UNDERSTANDING THE RAW IMAGE FORMAT

The RAW image format is available on many high-end digital cameras. When you capture images in RAW format, you capture the digital data initially recorded by your camera's image sensor, with no additional processing or compression. The amount of data in a RAW image results in a larger file size when compared to images captured with the JPEG format, but the RAW format gives you a wider range of color to work with. Images captured in RAW format have dazzling color and fine detail. Cameras capable of recording images in RAW format include software that enables you to view and process the image after downloading it to your computer. After processing the image, you can export it as a TIFF or JPEG file for further editing in your favorite image-editing application. The data captured by your camera in RAW mode enables you to create dazzling photographs, like the one shown here. Once the domain of professional photographers only, the RAW format is increasingly becoming an option for all levels of digital camera owners to consider in the proper circumstances. Photoshop CS2/CS3, Photoshop Lightroom, and Photoshop Elements 5 have camera RAW plug-ins that enable you to process the images and edit them in the same application.

TIFF files offer the best image quality from images that are processed in camera, while RAW offers the best overall quality. JPEG images are also processed in the camera and are compressed, resulting in smaller file sizes. In addition to image size, many digital cameras have a setting for image quality—the settings have names like "normal," "fine," and, with some cameras, "super-fine." High-quality images result in larger file sizes and sharper pictures. Many high-end cameras and most digital SLRs have a setting to capture images using the RAW format, which are read-only files that must be processed using a software application supplied by the camera manufacturer, or an image-editing application that supports the RAW file format. The RAW image is processed first and can be edited later.

Q: What camera features do I need?
A: The answer to this question depends on how you're going to use the camera. If you're a casual picture taker, you can probably get by with a point-and-shoot digital camera. Even the most basic point-and-shoot digital cameras have different shooting modes, and many come with features such as red-eye reduction. Basic point-and-shoot digital cameras generally offer 3 megapixel and higher resolution, which means you can get good-quality 5 × 7-inch images from the camera. However, if you're going to take a wide variety of pictures and want the most from your digital camera, you'll be happier with a high-end digital camera with a built-in wide angle to telephoto

zoom lens or a digital SLR. The following are a few features found on high-end cameras that you may want to consider:

- **Anti-dust systems** are found on some digital SLRs. These safeguard against dust buildup on the camera sensor, which often occurs when changing lenses. Anti-dust systems consist of a coating on the sensor that repels dust. The sensor is gently shaken when the camera is shut off to dislodge any dust that may have accumulated on the sensor.

- **Auto-exposure bracketing (AEB)** enables you to take three pictures of a scene: one with the camera's recommended setting, one with a higher exposure, and one with a lower exposure. This option ensures you'll get the same shot in difficult lighting conditions.

- **Exposure control** enables you to capture images in aperture priority mode or shutter priority mode, depending on the type of scene you are capturing. Many cameras also give you the option of setting the exposure manually. When you shoot in aperture priority mode, you can control how much light is let into the camera, which also determines how much of the scene is in focus (known as depth of field). When you shoot in shutter priority mode, the camera exposes the image based on the shutter speed you specify. A high shutter speed enables you to freeze action. If your camera has a manual mode, you set both shutter speed and aperture to arrive at the desired exposure.

- **Image stabilization** compensates for any operator movement while the camera is recording the image. This helps you get a sharper image when you're using maximum zoom and when shooting at slow shutter speeds. This option is especially useful on cameras with an optical zoom of 5X or greater. Image stabilization will compensate for operator movement, but not for movement of the subject. However, slight subject movement, such as the wave of a hand, which will show up as a soft blur, can add charm to a photo. As of this writing, Sony's Alpha (DSLR A100) and Pentax's K10D and K100D are the only digital SLRs with built-in camera image stabilization. Other digital SLR manufacturers offer lenses that have built-in image stabilization.

- **Movie mode** enables you to create movies with your digital camera. While a digital camera with movie mode is not a substitute for a digital video camera, this feature will enable you to create movies that can be viewed with the associated software on a computer monitor or from a Web site. Most digital cameras offer a movie mode that lets you create a movie at 15 fps (frames per second), while some high-end cameras offer 30 or 60 fps. The length of the movie you can capture depends on the camera firmware, which is software built into the camera that determines how much of the camera buffer is used to store images and movies being processed by it. If your camera's movie mode offers uninterrupted video, the length of the movie is determined

TIP

When changing the lens on a digital SLR, turn the power off and point the camera down.

TIP

Many camera features are accessed through the camera menu. Make sure the camera you're considering has an easy to read menu.

by the size of your memory card. Other cameras have a maximum of three minutes per recorded movie. Some cameras have built-in microphones that enable you to create a movie with sound.

- **Macro mode** enables you to take close-up images of objects such as flowers, jewelry, or watches.

- **Optical zoom of 5X or more** enables you to zoom in tight on a scene, which is useful when photographing wildlife from afar. A high level of optical zoom is the equivalent of having a 35-mm camera telephoto lens with a focal length of 180 mm or greater. For example, a Canon S3 IS camera lens has a maximum optical zoom of 12X, which is the 35-mm equivalent of a 432-mm lens.

- **Through-the-lens viewing** uses an electronic viewfinder that displays what the camera image sensor will record.

Q: What is meant by 35-mm equivalent?

A: The sensor on most digital cameras is smaller than the frame size of a 35-mm negative. Therefore, the image you get from a digital camera is cropped to a smaller area of the scene than would be recorded by a 35-mm camera with the same focal length lens. This is the equivalent of zooming in on a scene. You may see specifications that list a magnification factor for the sensor such as 1.3, 1.5, or 1.6. The 35-mm equivalent is the lens focal length, multiplied by the focal length multiplier. For example, if the focal length of a camera lens is 30 mm and the focal length multiplier of the sensor is 1.6, the 35-mm equivalent is 48 mm.

Q: How do I get the images into my computer?

A: You can download the images from your camera to your computer using the Universal Serial Bus (USB) cable supplied with most modern digital cameras, which you connect to a USB slot on your computer. Alternatively, you can purchase a card reader, which is also hooked to your computer via a USB cable, as shown in Figure 1-4. When you connect your digital camera to a computer or insert a memory card into a card reader that's connected to your computer, the computer recognizes the device, and you can download the images to the desired folder on your hard drive. After you download the images to your computer, you can edit them in your image-editing application to prepare them for viewing or optimize them for printing.

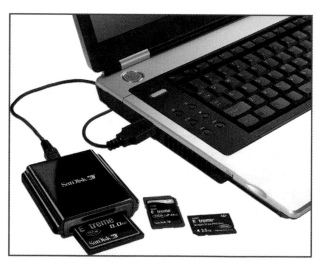

Figure 1-4: You can download images to your computer with a USB card reader.

Purchase a Digital Camera

Whether you're going to purchase your first digital camera or purchase a second digital camera with more powerful features, it's a good idea to do your homework first. If you rush out blindly and buy the first digital camera that looks cool or the one the friendly salesperson recommends, you may end up with a bad case of buyer's remorse when you actually use the camera.

Prepare a Needs List

Digital cameras are hot-ticket items, and there are all manner of makes and models available. If you prepare a list of your needs before shopping for your camera, you'll get exactly what you want and not succumb to slick advertising claims. If you buy a digital camera without knowing what you really need, you'll end up with either a camera that falls short of the mark or a high-priced camera with bells and whistles that you'll never use. Prepare your list by answering the following questions:

- **How often will you use the camera and what type of photographs will you take?** If you use a camera infrequently to capture only images of friends and family events, your best bet may be a point-and-shoot digital camera.

- **Will you be creating prints of your photographs?** If you plan to create prints of your photographs, consider purchasing a camera with a resolution of 5 megapixels or greater. The added resolution will enable you to print good-quality 8 × 10 images.

- **Will you be using the camera for wildlife photography?** If so, consider a model with a 5X or greater optical zoom. Another useful feature for wildlife photography is a camera that will shoot several frames per second and continually focus on wildlife as it moves toward and away from you. Image stabilization, which will enable you to get sharper images when using long focal lengths or when shooting in low-light conditions, is another option to consider.

TIP

If you wear glasses, opt for a camera with a large LCD monitor.

- **Will you be photographing in inclement conditions or while canoeing or kayaking?** If so, consider purchasing a camera that has a waterproof body. As of this writing, Bushnell, Olympus, and Pentax offer digital cameras with waterproof bodies. In fact, Pentax has a digital SLR with a waterproof body. Alternatively, you may be able purchase a waterproof housing for your camera, which enables you to shoot underwater.

- **Will you be photographing sporting events?** If so, your camera should have a sports shooting mode or allow you to select a shooting mode that gives you the option of setting the shutter speed, which enables you to freeze action such as athletes in motion. With a camera that enables you to manually set shutter speeds, another option to shoot with a slower shutter speed and pan to capture compelling images of fast-moving objects like race cars and motorcycles. The end result is a photograph that shows sharp detail on the moving object with a blurred background to give the viewer the sensation of speed.

- **Will you be photographing portraits of people?** If so, your camera needs a portrait mode. Better yet, the camera should have an aperture-preferred shooting mode and a fast telephoto lens with an aperture setting of f/2.8, which enables you to create a limited depth of field, where your subject is in clear focus, but the background and foreground are blurry.

- **Do you own a 3-5mm SLR film camera manufactured by Canon, Minolta, Nikon, or Pentax?** If you own a Canon, Nikon, or Pentax film camera, your auto-focus (AF) lenses may work with the manufacturer's digital SLR. If you own a Minolta film camera with A-mount lenses, they can be used with the Sony Alpha digital SLR.

- **Do you want the capability of editing your images after downloading them to your computer?** If so, your camera should include image-editing software. If the camera has Adobe Photoshop Elements, Corel Paint Shop Pro, or similarly powerful software, you can use these applications to color-correct, resize and crop images, and much more.

- **Do you want the capability of printing photo-quality prints of your images?** If so, your camera should be 4.0 megapixels or greater. A 4.0-megapixel camera in its best shooting mode will give you high-quality 4 × 6 inch prints; a 5.0-megapixel or better camera will yield images as large as 8 × 10 inches.

- **Will you be shooting in low light?** If so, your camera should offer the option to set the ISO rating. The camera should also have a maximum setting of ISO 400 or higher. Image stabilization is another handy option if you shoot in low light.

NOTE

Many cameras ship with proprietary software that doesn't give you a lot of power when it comes to editing images. The image-editing applications that will be discussed later in this book can be purchased from retail outlets and online.

RESEARCHING YOUR PURCHASE

After creating your list, you'll have the necessary information to search for a digital camera that matches your needs. After you find a camera that matches your needs, you may feel you're ready to purchase the camera. However, camera manufacturers have different ways of incorporating features with their products. Some implementations are innovative, while others fall far short of the mark. Before buying a camera, it's always a good idea to read what the experts have to say about the model.

With the information from your needs list, you're ready to find a camera that includes the features you need. Visit Web sites that provide news and reviews about current camera models. A couple of good Web sites to check out for this type of information are www.dpreview .com and www.cnet.com. This illustration shows an authoritative camera review from www.dpreview.com.

You can also visit your favorite search engine and type the keywords digital camera reviews for additional resources. After checking out the online camera reviews, you can then visit the manufacturer's Web site. The following list shows the types of cameras sold by major companies and the URLs for their Web sites.

- **Canon**   Point-and-shoot digital, high-end digital, digital SLR
  www.usa.canon.com/consumer/controller?act=ProductCatIndexAct&fcategoryid=113

- **Fujifilm**   Point-and-shoot digital, high-end digital, digital SLR
  www.fujifilm.com/products/digital/index.html

Continued . . .

- **Are you an experienced photographer?** If so, you're likely to shoot subjects that are backlit. Thus, your camera should have a mode for shooting in backlit situations. Better yet, the camera should have multiple metering modes.

- **Will you be capturing images of fast-moving objects?** If so, your camera should have a maximum shutter speed of 1/2000 of a second or more.

- **Do you want the capability of taking wide angle or telephoto shots beyond the range of the camera lens?** If so, your camera should have some method of accepting accessory lenses. Many high-end digital cameras have lens threads that enable you to attach an auxiliary wide-angle or telephoto lens. If you purchase a digital SLR camera, you can choose from a wide variety of manufacturer and after-market lenses in a wide range of focal lengths.

- **Do you wear glasses or have problems reading fine print?** If so, purchase a camera with the largest LCD monitor you can afford. This makes it easier to read the camera menus. Many cameras now sport a 2.5-inch or larger monitor.

QUICKSTEPS

RESEARCHING YOUR PURCHASE

(Continued)

- **Nikon**   Point-and-shoot digital, high-end digital, digital SLR
  http://nikonimaging.com/global/products/digitalcamera/index.htm

- **Olympus**   Point-and-shoot digital, high-end digital, digital SLR
  www.olympusamerica.com/cpg_section/cpg_digital.asp

- **Pentax**   Point-and-shoot digital, high-end digital, digital SLR
  www.pentaximaging.com/products/cameras/digital/

- **Sony**   Point-and-shoot digital, high-end digital, digital SLR
  www.sonystyle.com/is-bin/INTERSHOP.enfinity/eCS/Store/en/-/USD/SY_BrowseCatalog-Start?CategoryName=dcc_DIDigitalCameras&Dept=cameras

TIP

You can also find digital camera reviews in photography magazines. In fact, many magazines contain nothing but information and reviews about popular digital cameras and accessories. Your local bookstore probably has a section devoted to photography magazines.

Know Your Choices

After assessing your needs, the next step is to find the ideal camera with features that suit your needs and lifestyle. There are many types of digital cameras, and each one has a wide variety of models by various manufacturers. Figure 1-5 shows a few of the different types of digital cameras available from Canon and Sony. The following sections will give you an idea of the types of cameras that are available today.

Consider Point-and-Shoot Digital Cameras

If you take pictures infrequently but would still like the convenience of a digital camera, a point-and-shoot camera is ideal for you. Point-and-shoot cameras

Figure 1-5: Each camera manufacturer offers a wide variety of models.

TIP

Many cameras have a hard time focusing in low-light situations. You can overcome this obstacle by choosing a camera that gives you the ability to focus manually.

TIP

If you're considering a camera with a through-the-lens electronic viewfinder, point the camera toward a bright light source, and view the scene through the viewfinder. Some cameras with electronic viewfinders don't do a good job of displaying a brightly lit scene through the electronic eyepiece.

TIP

If you need a digital camera that's capable of zooming in tightly on a scene, always opt for a high degree of *optical* zoom. Many cameras offer *digital* zoom to augment the maximum focal length of the camera lens. When a camera is in digital zoom mode, however, the camera magnifies a small portion of the image, as recorded in maximum optical zoom, and then expands the image to a larger size, which results in a blockier image because there are fewer pixels with which to work.

are relatively easy to operate, and many feature up to 4X optical zoom. Some feature multiple shooting modes to compensate for lighting conditions and fast-moving objects. Most point-and-shoot cameras do not have a through-the-lens viewfinder. In this category, you'll find cameras that are small enough to fit in your shirt pocket, from low-megapixel cameras capable of creating wallet-sized prints, up to 5-megapixel cameras that enable you to create good-quality 8 × 10-inch prints. These cameras generally sell for less than $500.

Consider Prosumer Digital Cameras

If you're the creative type, who likes to take pictures you can frame and share with relatives and friends, consider purchasing a "prosumer" camera. Cameras in this category feature extended optical zoom up to 12X that enable you to creatively compose your scene and zoom in on faraway objects. Many cameras in this category feature through-the-lens viewing, which enables you to accurately compose a scene through the viewfinder. Most of these cameras feature multiple shooting modes, which you can use to control how much of the scene is in focus and to freeze the action. Prosumer cameras typically come with built-in zoom and through-the-lens viewfinders. Cameras in this category begin at the 7-megapixel level and sell for between $500 and $1000.

Consider Digital SLR

If you're an advanced hobbyist or a professional photographer making the switch to digital, a digital SLR is the logical camera to choose. Digital SLRs function just like their film-carrying brethren. In fact, if you currently own a 35-mm SLR, you may be able to use your current lenses with a digital SLR by the same manufacturer. Digital SLRs feature interchangeable lenses, on-camera flash, and advanced shooting modes that you can use to creatively photograph the world around you. Some digital SLRs feature anti-dust technology. As of this writing, Sony and Pentax are the first manufacturers to feature on-camera image-stabilization, which enables you to get sharp shots at slower shutter speeds. You can accessorize your camera by purchasing lenses, filters, off-camera flashes, and more. These cameras range in price from $700 to $4500.

Search for the Perfect Camera

The choice of which camera to use is highly subjective. You may be inclined to make your purchase as soon as you've completed your needs list and selected the ideal candidate after reading online reviews. You may also be tempted to find the lowest price online and order the camera directly. Even though the camera has the features you need and has received glowing reviews, it may not, however, be the right camera for you.

Try Before You Buy

The only way you can be sure if your candidate is indeed the ideal digital camera for you is to hold it in your hands and make sure the controls are logically placed and comfortable for you, that the camera is easy to use, and that it takes acceptable pictures. In other words, the only way you really can be sure that the camera is right for you is to try before you buy. Visit a local retailer that stocks your ideal camera. Ask the salesperson to let you hold the camera. Turn the camera on, and notice how long it takes the camera to power up. Look through the viewfinder, and press the shutter button halfway. Notice how quickly the camera focuses on the subject. If the camera takes more than three seconds to power up, or if it takes a second or two to focus, you may end up losing spontaneous shots.

Press the shutter button all the way to take a picture. Notice how long it takes the camera to record the picture. All digital cameras have shutter lag to some degree (the time it takes to record the picture after you press the shutter button). On some cameras, the lag is so short that it isn't noticeable. However, if the lag is excessive, you run the risk of not capturing quickly evolving action.

Put the camera through its paces by taking pictures of objects in the store. Use the camera zoom and flash to see how they perform. If the camera features a macro mode, take a close-up shot of your watch. Review the pictures you've just taken using the camera's built-in LCD monitor. Make sure the images are sharp and colorful. (The only true test of image quality is to view it on

TIP

If you're previewing the camera in a computer superstore, ask the salesperson to download the images to a computer, and preview them on-screen. However, don't expect the salesperson to accommodate your request if you visit the store on a day when they are busy.

a computer screen, but the LCD monitor may give you an idea of what the camera is capable of.) If the camera has controls that enable you to zoom in on an image when viewing it with the built-in monitor, do so, and make sure the details are clear and in focus. If possible, ask the salesperson to print one of the pictures. Examine the print for clarity, color, and sharpness.

All cameras have a feature that powers the camera down when it's not used for a period of time. Most cameras come back to life when you press the shutter button halfway. Notice how long it takes the camera to "wake up." If it takes more than a second, you may end up losing shots when action occurs that you want to capture. This is especially important if you photograph sporting events.

Choose Digital Film

Your camera's removable storage media is the digital equivalent of film. Most manufacturers include one removable storage media card with the camera, which, when the card is full of images, you can download to your computer. However, if you shoot lots of pictures when you travel and don't have access to a computer, you'll need additional cards. And if your camera does ship with a memory card, it's generally small and doesn't hold many images, especially if you shoot images using the camera's highest resolution.

The size of the digital media and the image quality you choose determines how many images you can store. If you own a high-end digital SLR that uses CompactFlash media, you may be able to benefit from the new super-size storage devices with capacities up to 16 GB. Table 1-1 shows the number of images you can fit on a 128-MB CompactFlash card. The information is based on an 8-megapixel Canon camera.

IMAGE SIZE/ QUALITY	IMAGE SIZE (PIXELS)	FILE FORMAT	COMPRESSION	FILE SIZE	CAPACITY
RAW	3264 × 2448	RAW	N/A	9.0 MB	13 images
Large/superfine Large/fine	3264 × 2448	JPEG	Low Medium	3.4 MB 2.1 MB	35 images 59 images
Medium/superfine Medium/fine	2272 × 1704		Low Medium	2.0 MB 1.1 MB	61 images 110 images
Medium 3/superfine Medium 3/fine	1024 × 768		Low Medium	570 KB 320 KB	215 images 379 images

Table 1-1: Image Capacity for 128-MB CompactFlash Card

QUICK**FACTS**

STEPPING UP TO ULTRA-FAST STORAGE MEDIA

If you own a high-end digital camera capable of recording multiple frames that includes other features, such as AEB, you may find that a standard memory card isn't up to the task. Standard memory cards were designed for point-and-shoot cameras. The read and write speeds of a standard memory card may not be fast enough to keep up with your high-end camera. When a memory card can't write the information fast enough, the data is stored in the camera's memory buffer and written to the memory card when available. You will not be able to record images when the camera's memory buffer is full.

If your camera uses CompactFlash, Memory Stick, Memory Stick Duo, or SD media, you'll be able to equip your camera with a fast memory card. SanDisk (www.sandisk.com) is one of the many manufacturers that offer a line of professional memory cards. SanDisk has professional memory cards in two series: Ultra, which has a read speed of 10 MB per second and a write speed of 9 MB per second, and Extreme III, which has read and write speeds of 20 MB per second. As an added bonus, the Extreme series of memory cards will work in temperatures from –13 degrees Fahrenheit to 185 degrees Fahrenheit. Sony offers fast media storage in the form of Memory Stick Pro for users of its digital cameras. The following illustration shows some of the high-performance memory cards you can purchase at your local retailer or online.

Accessorize Your Camera

When you purchase a point-and-shoot or high-end digital camera, you get just enough equipment to take pictures. Your digital camera may or may not come with a memory card. When you purchase a digital SLR, you often get just the body. Some retailers offer digital SLR kits that include a lens and perhaps a flash. Whatever type of camera you buy, you may find that you want to add a case, a tripod, or other items to improve the quality of your experience and the photos you take.

Purchase Extra Batteries and Memory Cards

There's nothing more frustrating then running out of battery power when you're in the middle of breathtaking scenery. And some cameras are notoriously hard on batteries. Whether your camera comes with a rechargeable lithium-ion battery or disposable batteries, consider purchasing an extra set. Another useful option is a battery charger that runs off a car cigarette lighter.

It's almost as frustrating to run out of storage space when you're taking photos. If your camera has a built-in storage device, it can be quickly filled when you're shooting interesting subjects. If your camera came with a removable storage device, it is probably woefully small. Therefore, another useful purchase is extra memory cards. Some camera dealers offer bundles with additional memory cards and other options.

Add Additional Lenses

If you own a high-end digital camera, you can purchase a wide angle or telephoto attachment to extend your picture-taking capabilities. High-end digital cameras usually feature accessory threads at the end of the lens. You simply screw the attachment into the threads, and take your picture. If you own a digital SLR, the sky's the limit. You can choose from

Figure 1-6: You have ultimate creative control when you accessorize your digital SLR with wide angle and telephoto lenses.

 TIP

Purchase a case that is water-repellent so you can protect your camera in inclement weather. Another useful feature is an internal waterproof pocket for storing memory cards.

Figure 1-7: A sturdy camera bag is a handy accessory to protect and house your camera and accessories.

a wide range of lenses supplied by the camera manufacturer or third-party lens manufacturers. You can purchase lenses from a local retailer or through Internet outlets. It's a good idea to try the lens before buying, especially if you're buying a lens manufactured by a third-party lens manufacturer. Figure 1-6 shows lenses available for a Sony digital SLR.

Protect Your Digital Camera with a Case

If you own a small point-and-shoot camera, you may be able to get by without a case. After all, most of them are small enough to fit in a shirt pocket. However, if you own a high-end digital camera or a digital SLR, you'll need space to store the camera and your accessories. A case also serves as protection when the weather is inclement.

When you purchase a case for your camera, choose one that is large enough for the camera and the accessories you now own, as well as for accessories that you are considering purchasing in the near future. You can purchase a camera case from a well-stocked retail outlet, a camera store, or an online camera store. Some camera cases are customizable, with removable partitions that attach to the case with Velcro. Lowepro (www.lowepro.com) is one manufacturer that offers a wide range of camera bags, from those that will fit the smallest point-and-shoot camera to those that house a digital SLR, complete with accessories and lenses. Many of the Lowepro bags have waterproof covers. Figure 1-7 shows examples of Lowepro camera bags for digital cameras.

Choose a Tripod

Most point-and-shoot digital cameras feature a tripod thread, and all high-end, zoom-lens reflex and digital SLR cameras have one. This enables you to secure the camera to a tripod. A tripod steadies the camera when you're taking a picture that requires a lengthy exposure. Figure 1-8 shows a tripod suitable for a lightweight digital camera.

If you own a digital SLR, note the weight of your camera before you purchase a tripod. (This isn't mandatory when you're buying a tripod for a point-and-shoot or lightweight high-end digital camera.) If you purchase a tripod that's not rated for the weight of your camera, it won't be stable enough to ensure that you get sharp pictures. Make sure to note the weight of the camera with your heaviest lens and external flash attached.

Decide which accessories you'd like on your tripod. A spirit level is a nice accessory, as it enables you to adjust the tripod so that the camera is perfectly level. A tripod case is another handy accessory.

Choose an External Flash

Many high-end digital cameras and all digital SLR cameras come with a hot shoe that enables you to attach an external flash to the camera. External flash units are more powerful than the ones built into digital cameras, and they present you with wonderful options, such as bounce lighting. Figure 1-9 shows external flash units that will work with Canon digital cameras.

Figure 1-8: Use a tripod to stabilize your camera when shooting at slow shutter speeds.

Figure 1-9: External flash units are more powerful than on-camera ones.

Add an External Storage Device

If you travel frequently and shoot lots of pictures during your trips, you'll need to invest in a lot of memory cards, carry a laptop computer with you, or purchase an external storage device (see Figure 1-10). External storage devices are battery-powered, and some feature a monitor that you can use to view your images. External storage devices work with most popular memory cards. You copy the images from your memory card to the storage device, which is usually a hard drive. There are also external storage devices that you can use to copy your images to a CD or DVD. After you download the images to the portable storage device, format the memory card and continue shooting. If you own two memory cards, you can use one to continue shooting pictures while the portable storage device is downloading your other memory card. After you return from your trip, connect the pocket hard drive to your computer and download the images.

Figure 1-10: Portable hard drives enable you to store images when your memory cards are full.

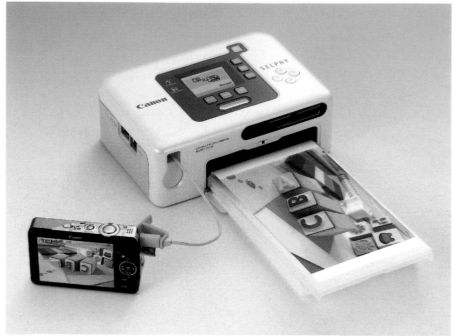

Figure 1-11: Many photo-quality printers enable you to create prints without a computer.

Purchase a Photo-Quality Printer

The popularity of digital photography has spawned a plethora of photo-quality printers. This is another case where it pays to do a bit of research and shopping before buying. Low-priced photo-quality printers are available with three color inks and one black, but the better models have six color inks and two black inks. Many photo-quality printers also have built-in card readers and small monitors that enable you to print images from your memory card without needing a computer, as shown in Figure 1-11. Visit a store that carries the printer you are interested in. Bring a memory card that holds some colorful photos you have taken, and ask the salesperson if you can test the printer by creating a couple of 4 × 6 prints of your images.

How to...

Chapter 2
Getting the Most from Your Camera

Digital cameras have different controls and settings from conventional film cameras. Many of the controls and settings are included in the camera's menu. While each camera is somewhat different, they do share similar controls and settings. Point-and-shoot digital cameras are the easiest to operate, while high-end and digital SLR (single lens reflex) cameras have more settings and controls. In this chapter, you'll learn the basics of taking pictures with a digital camera.

Take Photographs with Your Digital Camera

Digital photography is all about instant gratification. No matter what type of digital camera you own, you don't have to wait for prints to be processed before you know whether or not you got the shot. A second or so after you take the

Camera mode dial

Figure 2-1: You can choose the camera mode to suit the subject you're photographing or the conditions in which you're photographing.

picture, it appears on the camera's LCD monitor. If you don't like what you see, delete it. The following sections describe how to capture images using the different types of digital cameras on the market. You'll also learn specific techniques to get the most from your digital camera in the latter parts of this chapter.

Use a Point-and-Shoot Digital Camera

When you use a point-and-shoot camera, the camera takes care of pretty much everything for you, with the exception of choosing the subject and composing the picture. However, even the simplest point-and-shoot camera is equipped with a dial that enables you to choose different shooting modes (as shown in Figure 2-1) to compensate for backlit subjects, fast-moving subjects, and so on.

1. Turn the camera mode dial to select the desired shooting mode.

2. Compose your picture through the viewfinder or LCD viewer. If desired, use your camera's zoom control to zoom in on your subject and achieve the perfect composition.

3. Press the shutter button halfway to focus on your center of interest. Most cameras will flash a green dot while focusing. When the dot stops flashing, focus has been achieved. You may also hear a beep.

4. Press the shutter to take the picture. After you take the picture, you may see an hourglass or some other symbol that signifies that the camera is processing the picture. A short while later, the processed picture appears in the LCD viewer.

Shoot Pictures with a High-End Digital Camera

If you own a high-end digital camera, you can exercise creative control over your pictures. In addition to shooting modes that compensate for lighting conditions and fast-moving objects, you have an aperture-priority shooting mode, shutter-priority shooting mode, and manual shooting mode. Most high-end cameras feature a zoom lens with a wide range of focal lengths and enable you to view the image through an electronic viewfinder that shows you exactly what will be recorded by the camera's image sensor. These cameras are similar

Figure 2-2: High-end digital cameras often feature a high optical zoom.

to digital SLRs, but have non-removable lenses. Figure 2-2 shows a high-end digital camera that features an electronic viewfinder and focal lengths that range from 36 mm to 432 mm (35-m equivalent).

1. Turn the camera mode dial to the desired shooting mode. If you choose one of the preset modes, go to step 4.

2. If desired, select the metering mode. Most high-end digital cameras have three metering modes: evaluative (also known as matrix or multipattern) metering, center-weighted, and spot metering (also known as partial metering). You'll learn how to select the proper metering mode for the conditions under which you are shooting in the section "Choose the Proper Metering Mode."

3. If you choose a creative mode, you'll have to adjust either the shutter speed when shooting in shutter priority mode (listed on most camera dials as Tv, an abbreviation for "time value," or S for "shutter") or the aperture when shooting in aperture priority mode (listed on most camera dials as Av, an abbreviation for "aperture value," or A for "aperture"). If you're shooting in manual mode, which is listed as M on most cameras, you adjust both the shutter speed and aperture to achieve the desired exposure.

4. Compose your scene through the viewfinder or LCD viewer. Most high-end cameras feature an electronic through-the-lens viewfinder, which allows you to accurately compose the scene based on what the image sensor is recording. Some photographers prefer to compose their pictures using the LCD monitor.

5. Press the shutter button halfway to achieve focus. The camera gives you a visual indication in the viewfinder or LCD monitor when focus has been achieved. You may also hear a beep, depending on the model of the camera.

6. Press the shutter button fully to take the picture. Modern high-end cameras respond quickly. You'll see the processed image in the LCD viewer almost immediately.

Shoot Images with a Digital SLR

When you shoot images with a digital SLR, you have the utmost in creative freedom. You can capture images with a wide array of lenses—everything from a super wide-angle fish-eye lens to a long telephoto lens with a focal length of 500 mm or greater. You can use a wide-angle lens to record a picturesque landscape and then quickly change to a telephoto lens to capture a close-up of a distant animal. Figure 2-3 shows two shots of a digital SLR, one with a

Figure 2-3: With a digital SLR, you choose the proper lens for the subject.

super wide zoom lens attached and one with a telephoto zoom lens attached.

1. Select the proper lens for the scene you are going to capture, and swap it with the current lens.

2. Turn the camera mode dial to select the desired shooting mode. If you choose one of the creative modes, you'll need to adjust the shutter speed, aperture, or both. Creative modes are covered in detail in the section "Shoot Images Using Creative Shooting Modes."

3. Choose the proper metering mode for the scene. Metering modes will be covered in detail in the section "Choose the Proper Metering Mode."

4. Compose the scene through the camera viewfinder. With a digital SLR, you're looking right through the lens, so what you see is what you get.

5. Press the shutter button halfway to achieve focus. The camera will flash a visual warning in the viewfinder when focus has been achieved. Your camera may also beep when focus is achieved.

6. Press the shutter button fully to take the picture. Soon you'll see the image on the camera's LCD viewer.

TIP

For images you're going to e-mail, you can get by with an image size as low as 640 × 480 pixels. Choose normal image quality mode.

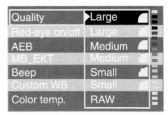

Figure 2-4: You use the camera menu to specify image size and quality.

Utilize All of Your Camera's Features

Whether you own the simplest point-and-shoot digital camera, a sophisticated high-end digital camera, or a digital SLR, you'll get better pictures if you learn to utilize all of your camera's features. Your camera has controls that you can use to gain control of the picture-taking process—for example, in difficult lighting conditions, such as photographing a person on a brightly lit beach. Your camera also has controls that determine image size and quality.

Set Image Size and Quality

1. Power up your camera.

2. Press the menu button.

3. Navigate to the menu item that determines image size and quality.

4. Select the desired image size and quality. Figure 2-4 shows the image size and quality menu for a Canon digital SLR.

QUICKSTEPS

SAVING THE MAXIMUM NUMBER OF IMAGES TO YOUR MEMORY CARD

The file size of an image is determined by the image size and quality you specify. If you own a high-megapixel camera and shoot at the largest image size and best quality, your image file sizes will be quite large. If you don't have spare memory cards or a device to download the images to, your memory card may run out of room. You can conserve space on your memory card by choosing a smaller image size and lower quality for the images you'll share via e-mail, because they don't need the same high resolution as images you'll print. You can also gain additional space on a memory card by deleting unwanted images. However, deleting images does sap battery power. Some digital cameras are notoriously hard on batteries, so delete images with caution. Delete unwanted images only if you have a spare battery on hand, or if you have plenty of power left in the camera battery.

CONSERVE YOUR MEMORY CARD

1. Monitor the number of images you'll be able to save to your memory card. Digital cameras have some means of displaying the number of images captured and the remaining number of images that can be saved to the card. Refer to your camera manual for further information.

2. Press the camera menu button.

3. Navigate to the image size and quality section of your menu.

4. Choose a smaller image size and quality.

Match the Metering Mode to Conditions

If you own a high-end digital camera or a digital SLR, you can choose the metering mode that best suits the conditions under which you are shooting the picture. The subject matter also plays a part in the metering mode you choose. Camera manufacturers refer to metering modes by different names. The most common designations and their descriptions are listed in Table 2-1.

Choose the Proper Metering Mode

1. Analyze the scene through the viewfinder. If the scene has even lighting, you should use evaluative metering (some camera manufacturers refer to this mode as matrix or

METERING MODE	DESCRIPTION	METERING MODE ICON
Evaluative, matrix, or multipattern	Multipattern metering (also called evaluative or matrix metering) is a good choice for many shots, and may be suitable for backlit subjects if the light source does not put the subject in heavy shade. The scene is metered from multiple metering zones, which are linked and averaged to determine the exposure for the scene.	◉
Center-weighted average	Use this mode when the background is significantly brighter than the subject. The scene is metered from a small area around the center of the scene.	□
Partial or spot	Use this mode when your subject is in the center of the scene. The metering is weighted toward the center of the scene and averaged for the entire scene.	⊙

Table 2-1: Matching the Metering Mode to Scene Conditions

multipattern metering). If you're photographing a person or subject in front of a bright light source, such as the sun, you should use the center-weighted average metering mode. If your subject is the most important part of the scene, use partial metering (some camera manufacturers refer to this mode as spot metering), and make sure you aim the metering mode icon in the center of your camera viewfinder at your subject.

2. Press the button or make the menu choice for the desired metering mode. Refer to your camera manual for detailed information on changing metering modes.

3. Compose the picture.

4. Press the shutter button halfway to focus the scene.

5. Press the shutter button fully to take the picture.

Lock Exposure

When you compose a photograph, you have a center of interest. This is the point of the photograph to which you want to draw the viewer's attention. Inexperienced photographers have a bad habit of placing the subject in the center of a scene, which can often lead to a boring photograph. Experienced photographers often compose a picture where the center of interest is off-center. If you compose pictures where your main subject is not centered in the viewfinder, you'll have to lock focus and exposure on the off-center subject using the auto-focus point, and then compose the picture. Most cameras provide a method for locking exposure to the auto-focus point.

Shoot an Off-Center Subject

1. Position the camera so that the subject is in the center of the viewfinder.

2. Push the shutter button halfway to lock focus and exposure. Note that some cameras require that you press a button to lock exposure on an off-center subject. Refer to your camera manual for more details.

3. Continue to hold the shutter button halfway and compose the scene.

4. Press the shutter button fully to record the image.

Focus the Scene

When you press the shutter button halfway, your camera focuses on a subject in your scene that intersects one of the auto-focus points. Most cameras have multiple auto-focus points. Your camera may have the option to switch to a single auto-focus point, in which case the camera will focus on the object nearest to the single auto-focus point you've selected. High-end digital cameras and digital SLR cameras usually have two auto-focus modes: a one-shot mode for still subjects and a mode where the camera focuses continuously on a moving subject.

Select an Auto-Focus Mode

1. Press your camera's focus mode button.
2. Choose the desired auto-focus mode. Alternatively, you may need to use the camera menu to change focus modes. Refer to your camera manual for detailed instructions.
3. Compose and shoot the picture.

Focus On an Off-Center Subject

1. Switch to a single focus point. Most cameras give you the option of switching to a single focus point in the center of the viewfinder.
2. Position your camera so that the subject you want in focus intersects the focus point.
3. Press the shutter button halfway to achieve focus.
4. Compose the scene with the shutter button still pressed halfway.
5. Press the shutter button fully to record the picture.

Use Preset Shooting Modes

When you shoot a picture using your camera's automatic mode, the camera exposes the picture based on the scene lighting, the objects in the scene, and the scene colors. This mode works well for average conditions. However, when you're shooting pictures in adverse lighting conditions or shooting pictures of fast-moving objects, you'll have to switch to one of your camera's preset modes. Table 2-2 lists the shooting modes you're likely to find on your camera mode dial.

TIP

Many cameras offer the option of switching to a single auto-focus point. This is useful when photographing a person. Switch to a center auto focus point, and aim that point at the person's head. Press the shutter halfway to achieve focus, and then compose and shoot the picture. The person's face will be in perfect focus in the resulting image.

TIP

If the camera is unable to achieve focus in low light conditions, momentarily shine a penlight on the area you want the camera to focus on. After focus has been achieved, turn off the penlight and take the picture. Alternatively, you can switch to manual focus.

TIP

Your camera may also have a mode that switches between one-shot focus and continuous focus. Continuous focus is handy when you're photographing moving objects.

SHOOTING MODE	DESCRIPTION	ICON
Close-up or macro	Enables you to shoot close-ups of subjects like flowers and butterflies.	
Portrait	Blurs the background to make the subject of your portrait the center of attention.	
Landscape	Used for scenic shots. The camera chooses a lens aperture that keeps both near and distant objects in focus.	
Sports	The camera selects a high shutter speed to freeze fast-moving objects and, when the shutter button is pressed halfway, continually focuses on the moving object.	
Night portrait (or slow synch)	Uses the flash to illuminate your subject and leaves the shutter open to record the ambient scenery. You should mount your camera on a tripod when using this mode, as the slow shutter speed may cause blurring. Your subject should remain perfectly still during the exposure. Note that with some cameras, you access this shooting mode through a menu command.	

Table 2-2: Choosing a Shooting Mode to Suit Your Scene

TIP

Remember to check your camera dial when you take the next picture to ensure that you're working with the desired shooting mode. For example, if you switch to portrait mode when shooting a portrait of someone and forget to change your camera dial to landscape when photographing a landscape, you'll ruin the picture.

Select a Shooting Mode

1. Analyze the scene to determine if you need to switch from automatic mode.

2. Select the desired shooting mode from your camera's shooting mode dial. Figure 2-5 shows the shooting mode dial for a Canon digital camera.

3. Compose and shoot the picture.

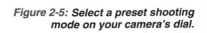

Figure 2-5: Select a preset shooting mode on your camera's dial.

Figure 2-6: You can use menu commands to enhance images and apply special effects.

Enhance Images with Camera Controls

Many digital cameras are equipped with menu options that enable you to enhance images. If your camera is so equipped, you can change image sharpness, contrast, and saturation. Your camera may also feature a camera setting to take pictures in black and white or settings that enable you to create special-effects images, such as sepia-toned photos. Consult your owner's manual to see which menu command is used to set each of these. Figure 2-6 (top) shows an image shot with the sharpness, contrast, and saturation set to their minimum values; Figure 2-6 (middle) shows an image shot with default settings for sharpness, contrast, and saturation; and Figure 2-6 (bottom) shows an image shot with maximum settings for sharpness, contrast, and saturation.

Shoot Images Using Creative Shooting Modes

High-end digital cameras and digital SLR cameras give you the option of shooting images using "creative" shooting modes. When you shoot using one of the creative shooting modes (aperture priority, shutter priority, and, with some cameras, program mode), you use the camera controls to create the desired image. When you shoot in aperture priority mode, you set the f-stop, which determines how much of the image is in focus (depth of field). When you shoot in shutter priority mode, you choose the desired shutter speed to freeze action or creatively blur the image. When you shoot in aperture priority mode, you select the desired aperture and the camera sets the shutter speed; in shutter priority mode, you select the desired shutter speed and the camera sets the aperture.

Capture Images Using Aperture Priority Mode

1. Turn the camera's mode dial to the aperture priority icon. Many cameras use the abbreviation Av or A for aperture priority mode.

2. Choose the desired f-stop. Refer to your camera manual for the control that sets the f-stop. If you select an f-stop that will result in an underexposed or overexposed picture, your camera will display a warning. Refer to your camera manual for further details.

3. Compose and shoot the picture.

Understand Lens f-Stops

The aperture setting is known as the f-stop. The lowest number f-stop lets the most amount of light reach the image sensor, the next f-stop lets half as much light reach the sensor, and so on. You control depth of field with f-stops. When you choose a low f-stop, such as f/2.8, more light reaches the image sensor and the depth of field is limited; objects behind your subject and in the foreground are blurry, as shown in Figure 2-7. A low f-stop is ideal for portraits. Notice how your attention is drawn to the model, while the background is a colorful blur. When you choose a high f-stop number, such as f/16, less light reaches the image sensor and more of your image is in focus, which is desirable when you're shooting a landscape, as shown in Figure 2-8. Notice how the entire image is sharp, from the dead Jeffrey pine in the foreground to the mountains in the distance.

Figure 2-7: Shoot with a low f-stop to blur the background when shooting portraits.

Figure 2-8: Shoot with a high f-stop when shooting subjects like landscapes.

Capture Images Using Shutter Priority Mode

1. Turn the camera's mode dial to the shutter priority icon. Many cameras use the abbreviation Tv or S for shutter priority mode.

2. Choose the desired shutter speed. Refer to your camera manual for the control that sets the shutter speed. If you select a shutter speed that will result in an underexposed or overexposed picture, your camera will display a warning. Refer to your camera manual for further details.

3. Compose and shoot the picture.

Understand Shutter Speeds

The shutter speed determines how long the shutter remains open to record the scene. Shutter speeds are measured in fractions of a second or, when shooting a long exposure, in seconds. If you're shooting in dim conditions without a flash, you'll need a slow shutter speed, such as 1/15 of a second. The rule of thumb for the slowest shutter speed at which you can handhold a camera is the reciprocal of the lens focal length (this refers to the 35-mm equivalent). In other words, if you're shooting an image with a digital SLR using a 20-mm lens with a focal length multiplier of 1.5, you'll need a tripod with any shutter speed slower than 1/30 of a second. You can, however, use a slow shutter speed to create artistic blurs, such as the headlight patterns shown in Figure 2-9. Slow shutter speeds are also useful

Figure 2-9: When you shoot at a slow shutter speed, you can create artistic blurs, such as headlight patterns.

Figure 2-10: Shoot at a high shutter speed to freeze action.

when photographing a stationary subject in dim lighting conditions. If you're photographing a subject with a slow shutter speed, your subject must remain perfectly still; otherwise, the image will be blurred. When you shoot at a high shutter speed, such as 1/2000 of a second, you freeze action, as shown in Figure 2-10. To avoid blurry images when you're using a high-end digital camera with a zoom lens, you'll need to shoot with a faster shutter speed when you zoom in tightly on a subject. When in doubt, a tripod will always ensure that the camera remains steady while you're taking the picture.

If your camera features image stabilization, be sure to enable the feature when taking photos that must be sharp. With image stabilization, you can shoot a couple of f-stops lower than you normally would. Remember, the general rule of thumb is that the slowest shutter speed you can use for the 35-mm equivalent of the focal length with which you're shooting is to use the reciprocal of the focal length. To find out how many stops lower you can shoot, enable image stabilization, and take several photographs of the same subject using slower shutter speeds than normal. Download the images to your computer, and compare them at 100 percent magnification. Examine the edges of objects in the scene for sharpness. This will tell you how many stops lower you can shoot than indicated by the reciprocal of the focal length, as discussed in the last paragraph.

CAUTION

Some cameras have an auto-ISO setting, which means that the camera chooses the ISO. Using this setting can cause unpredictable results. Your best bet is to choose the lowest ISO setting that enables you to create the desired rendition of the scene. In some instances, such as when photographing a landscape in cloudy conditions, you may have to use a tripod to shoot with a high f-stop to achieve the desired depth of field at a lower ISO setting.

Choose the ISO Setting

With a traditional film camera, you choose the film speed to match the conditions under which you'll be shooting: you use low-speed film in bright light or high-speed film in dim light. Most digital cameras and all digital SLR cameras enable you to choose the ISO setting to suit the scene you are recording, which is like changing film speed on-the-fly. For example, if you're inside a museum that prohibits flash photography, you can choose a higher ISO setting that enables you to shoot at a higher shutter speed to avoid camera blur.

DEALING WITH DIGITAL NOISE

If you capture pictures using ISO settings higher than ISO 400, you may notice digital noise in the form of colored specks in the picture. This is most noticeable when images are viewed at 100 percent magnification. Cameras with high ISO ratings usually have a noise reduction feature you can access via a menu command. Refer to your camera manual to see if your camera has this feature.

REDUCE DIGITAL NOISE

1. Select the desired ISO setting from your camera menu.

2. Select the noise filter option from your camera menu.

3. Compose and shoot the picture.

TIP

If your camera doesn't have a digital noise filter, mount your camera on a tripod, and shoot several pictures in low light without a flash. The ideal test of a camera's ability to deal with digital noise is a night scene with bright lights and a dark sky. Shoot the first picture at the lowest ISO setting, the second picture at the next highest ISO setting, and so on. Download the pictures to your computer, and preview them at 200 percent magnification to see the ISO setting at which digital noise becomes visible.

The ISO setting determines how sensitive the camera is to light. Choose a low ISO setting when shooting in bright light and a high ISO setting when shooting in dim light. ISO settings for digital cameras range from ISO 50 to ISO 3200, with a few offering ISO 6400. As mentioned previously, images captured with high ISO settings will have more digital noise. Some images photographed at ISO 3200 and ISO 6400 may be unusable due to the high degree of digital noise. Consult your camera manual for the available ISO range.

Increase Camera Sensitivity

1. Press your camera's menu button. Alternatively, certain cameras have a button devoted to accessing camera functions or adjusting the ISO setting.

2. Select the desired ISO setting.

3. Compose and shoot the picture.

Zoom In on Your Subject

Every digital camera features a zoom lens of some sort. Point-and-shoot digital cameras generally feature an optical zoom with a maximum magnification of 3X or 5X, while high-end digital cameras may have a zoom with a magnification as high as 12X. Your camera may also have digital zoom. Images captured with digital zoom are coarser than images captured with optical zoom. When you use digital zoom, the camera crops to an area of the maximum optical zoom and then enlarges it to the specified image size.

Use Optical Zoom

1. Point the camera toward the subject.

2. Press the zoom button to zoom in on the subject.

3. Compose and shoot the picture.

Use Digital Zoom

1. Point your camera toward the subject.

2. Press the zoom button until the maximum optical zoom has been achieved.

TIP

Many cameras with a high level of optical zoom have some sort of image stabilization feature. Use image stabilization when you are zooming in tightly on a subject to prevent blur from camera operator movement. You should also use a higher shutter speed when zooming to maximum magnification.

NOTE

Some cameras have a menu option to enable digital zoom. Refer to your camera manual for additional information.

3. Continue to press the zoom button to activate digital zoom.

4. Zoom in to the desired magnification.

5. Compose and shoot the picture.

Cope with Lighting Conditions

When objects are viewed in different lighting conditions, the three primary colors (red, green, and blue) exist in varying proportions, depending on the color temperature of the light source. As the color temperature changes, the color cast changes. When a color temperature is high, there is more blue. When the color temperature is low, there is more red. The human eye compensates for color temperature. When you view a white object under a fluorescent light, it appears white. However, the same object has a greenish cast when recorded by a camera image sensor. Your camera probably has AWB (automatic white balance), which compensates for color temperature under most conditions. However, if you notice that your images have a color cast, as shown in Figure 2-11 (left), you'll have to manually set the white balance using your camera menu settings. Figure 2-11 (right) shows the same subject with the white balance adjusted properly.

Figure 2-11: You can set white balance to suit lighting conditions.

NOTE

Some cameras have an external button to set white balance. Refer to your camera manual for detailed instructions on setting white balance for your camera.

TIP

Some cameras give you the option to create a custom white-balance setting by photographing a white piece of paper and then using a menu command to calibrate the camera's white balance based on the image you just photographed. Refer to your camera manual for additional details.

QUICKSTEPS

MAXIMIZING CAMERA BATTERY LIFE

As you gain experience with your digital camera, you'll use it more often and shoot more pictures in a single setting. Battery life varies, depending on the model of the camera you own and the number of features you use. For example, if your camera has image stabilization, more power is used when you enable the feature. When you power up the camera, an icon appears that indicates the state of the battery charge. Most cameras issue some kind of warning when you're about to exhaust the battery. There's nothing more frustrating than running out of battery power when you're photographing beautiful scenery. If your camera uses alkaline batteries, carry a spare set with you. If your camera uses a rechargeable lithium ion battery, purchase an extra battery and keep the fully charged spare in your camera bag.

Continued . . .

Set White Balance

1. Access your camera menu.
2. Choose the white balance setting to suit your scene. Table 2-3 shows the most common white balance settings and the icons you're likely to find on your camera (your camera may have slightly different icons). Refer to your camera manual for specific instructions on setting white balance.

WHITE BALANCE SETTING	ICON
Outdoors, sunny daylight, noon	
Outdoors, open shade	
Cloudy, hazy conditions	
Tungsten light	
Fluorescent light	
Camera flash	

Table 2-3: Choosing the proper white balance setting.

Get the Most from Your Digital Camera

After you gain experience in photography, you'll probably branch out and use your camera more creatively. For example, when taking portraits, you'll rotate the camera 90 degrees to capture a head and shoulders portrait, or head shot.

UICKSTEPS

MAXIMIZING CAMERA BATTERY LIFE *(Continued)*

Another option you may want to consider is a battery charger that works off a car cigarette lighter. That way, you can recharge an exhausted battery and shoot pictures with your spare. You can also change certain menu settings and do other things to maximize the life of your battery.

CONSERVE THE CAMERA BATTERY

1. Access your camera menu, and change the following settings:

   • Set the image review to the shortest interval. This determines the amount of time an image is displayed after you take a picture. Shorter review times conserve battery power.

   • Set the power-saving mode to the shortest interval. This determines the amount of time before the camera goes into sleep mode, which conserves battery power.

2. Whenever possible, use the camera viewfinder to compose your scene, as the LCD viewer uses more power.

3. Don't erase an image unless absolutely necessary. Erasing images consumes battery power.

4. Use your camera's zoom feature sparingly. The motor to power the camera's zoom uses battery power.

5. Only use the camera flash when necessary. If you get in the habit of shooting with natural light, you'll conserve battery power and get more natural-looking pictures to boot.

6. When shooting in cold climates, keep your camera warm when not in use. One method is to store the camera between your body and coat.

Your camera may have an option to auto-rotate images taken in portrait format 90 degrees. Your camera may also have the option to record movies. The size and frame rate of movies varies, depending on the camera model. Most digital cameras record movies with a frame size of 320 × 240 pixels and a frame rate of 15 to 30 fps (frames per second), while high-end digital cameras may feature the option to record movies with a frame size of 640 × 480, with a frame rate of up to 60 fps. You can use short movies in this format for e-mail attachments or for viewing on Web sites.

Auto-Rotate Images

1. Access your camera menu.
2. Navigate to the auto-rotate feature.
3. Enable the option.

Shoot Movies with Your Digital Camera

1. Turn your camera's mode dial to the movie icon. Figure 2-12 shows the camera mode dial for a Canon digital camera.
2. If applicable, use your camera menu to select the frame size and frame rate. Refer to your camera manual for detailed information on these settings.

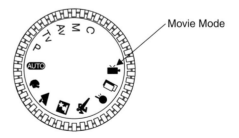

Movie Mode

Figure 2-12: Most point-and-shoot digital cameras have a mode for recording movies.

If your camera runs on conventional AA batteries, you may be able to use rechargeable batteries in your camera. Lots of rechargeable batteries are on the market. In fact, some manufacturers make batteries that will recharge in as little as 15 minutes. If you use rechargeable batteries, however, make sure this won't void your camera warranty.

TIP

Battery life is shorter when you're shooting in a cold climate. Keep your spare battery in your pocket to keep it warm. If you're not going to use your camera for a few weeks, remove the battery to prevent trickle discharge.

TIP

When traveling in a car, always secure your camera. If you have to brake suddenly, and the camera is not secure, it will continue moving at the speed of the car until it strikes something solid, like the dashboard, which can severely damage the sensitive circuitry in your camera. If you're traveling alone, place your camera bag in the passenger's seat and secure it with the seatbelt. If you own a point-and-shoot camera that you house in a small case, keep the camera in your glove box or some other location in the car where it won't become airborne if you have to suddenly brake. Another alternative is to hook the camera strap around the head rest.

3. Press the record button to begin recording your movie.

4. Press the record button again to stop recording your movie.

Maintain Your Digital Camera

Digital cameras are more complex and more expensive than their film-dependent brethren. You can lengthen the life of your equipment and ensure that the camera remains in peak operating condition if you follow a few simple steps.

Maintain Your Equipment

1. Clean the camera body with a soft cloth or microfiber cloth. Never use any solvents on the camera body.

2. Clean the camera viewfinder with a blower brush to remove dust and debris. Then wipe the viewfinder clean with a microfiber cloth.

3. Clean the camera lens with a blower brush to remove loose dust and debris. Gently wipe the lens with a microfiber cloth. If you own a digital SLR, remember to clean the rear element of each lens you own, as well as the front element. Many camera stores sell digital camera cleaning kits like the one shown in Figure 2-13.

Figure 2-13: You can purchase kits to maintain your digital camera.

Clean a Digital SLR Image Sensor

If you own a digital SLR and notice what looks like dust specks on your images, you may need to clean your camera's sensor. Clean the camera's image sensor by removing the lens and then using a menu command to flip up the mirror. While the mirror is locked in the upward position, use a gentle burst of air from a blower to dislodge any dust that may have accumulated on the image sensor when you changed lenses. Do not touch the image sensor with the blower. Never use a compressed air canister to clean the image sensor, because compressed air canisters contain liquid propellants that will be blown onto the image sensor and foul it. If you foul the image sensor with a liquid, you'll have to take your camera to a camera store to have it professionally cleaned. Refer to your camera manual for detailed instructions on cleaning your camera's image sensor.

There are also kits with swabs and chemicals that are used to professionally clean sensors. If you decide to use sensor cleaning swabs make sure they are of the highest quality and are specifically designed for the purpose of cleaning camera sensors. Sensor cleaning swabs are non-abrasive. To clean a sensor with a swab, you wet it with the solution, and then gently pass it over the sensor from edge to edge without touching the DSLR chamber. There are also brushes that can be used to clean camera sensors. The VisibleDust Arctic Butterfly® sensor brush shown in the image to the left is battery powered. To clean a sensor with the brush, prior to inserting the brush in the camera, you push a button, which spins the brush and charges it. You then gently rub the brush over the sensor taking care not to touch the sensor chamber. The charge attracts the dust particles to the brush, which once you remove the brush from the camera are expelled by pushing the button, which spins the brush. Beware of companies selling "artist" brushes for sensor cleaning. Artist brushes sweep the dust off the sensor and you run the risk of scratching the sensor.

Protect Your Camera Lens

If you own a digital SLR, consider purchasing a skylight or UV (*ultraviolet*) filter for each lens you own, and leave it on the lens at all times. The filters are relatively inexpensive and will protect the front lens element from damage. Note that the skylight filter will introduce a slight color cast, which will make the image warmer. If this is objectionable, use a UV filter to protect your lens. The skylight filter screws into the front of the lens, as shown in this illustration:

How to...

Chapter 3
Shooting Like a Pro

Anybody can take a photograph by pointing a camera at something and pressing the shutter button. However, to take a good photograph requires a bit of skill, thought, and creativity. There are several time-honored rules for taking photographs. In this chapter, you'll learn some of these rules, as well as other techniques for taking pictures like a pro.

Take Pictures Like a Pro

When you become proficient with your camera and its controls, you'll be ready to take your photography to the next level. You can create compelling photographs with your digital camera suitable for framing. In this chapter, you'll learn several techniques for taking professional-quality images.

Every rule is made to be broken. Before you take a photograph, examine the scene from several vantage points to determine the best composition. In most instances, the Rule of Thirds is the way to go, but other images are better when shot from straight on. If you have sufficient room on your memory card, shoot the same scene from several different angles.

QUICKSTEPS

MATCHING YOUR COMPOSITION TO THE SCENE

Beginning photographers rarely think of rotating the camera. However, if your subject is vertical, rotating the camera 90 degrees will give you a more interesting composition. For example, if you're photographing a tall waterfall or shooting a head-and-shoulders portrait, rotating the camera 90 degrees, which is known as portrait mode, guarantees you a more interesting image.

ROTATE THE CAMERA

1. Analyze the objects in your scene.

2. Rotate the camera 90 degrees if your subject is vertical. The image shows Bridal Veil Falls in Yosemite National Park as photographed with the camera rotated 90 degrees.

Compose the Photograph

1. Preview the scene through your viewfinder or LCD monitor.

2. Be aware of any obvious problems, like garbage cans in the background. Also be on the lookout for trees or telephone poles that appear to be growing out of your subject's head. If you have the time, move around the scene and photograph it from several angles. If you get in the habit of observing everything that's in the viewfinder, your composition skills will improve and your pictures will look more professional. After a while, observing subtle details will become second-nature.

3. Imagine a grid of nine squares over your scene, and place your center of interest where two gridlines intersect. This is known as the Rule of Thirds. The image in Figure 3-1 was composed with the cellist as the center of interest.

4. Focus on your center of interest. For more information on focusing, see Chapter 2.

5. Shoot the picture.

Figure 3-1: Compose your photograph to lead your viewer's eye to a center of interest.

Use Selective Focus

Another important decision you make when taking a photograph is how much of the scene will be in focus. If you're photographing a landscape, you want everything in the scene to be in focus; when photographing a person or group of people, you don't want the background to distract from the subject matter. If you have a camera capable of capturing images in aperture priority mode, you determine how much of the scene is in apparent focus (known as depth of field) by choosing the proper f-stop. If you have a point-and-shoot camera, you can determine how much of the scene is in focus by choosing the proper shooting mode. For more information on f-stops and depth of field, see Chapter 2.

Determine the Depth of Field

1. Switch to aperture-priority shooting mode.

2. Analyze the scene through your camera's viewfinder or LCD viewer.

3. Rotate the control on your camera that sets the f-stop. Select an f-stop of f /11 or higher (small aperture) when photographing a landscape, as shown in Figure 3-2. Select the lowest f-stop number (large aperture) when photographing a person, as shown in Figure 3-3.

4. If you're using a point-and-shoot camera that doesn't have an aperture priority mode, switch to landscape mode to maintain a large depth of field; switch to portrait mode to maintain a shallow depth of field, where only your main subject is in focus.

Figure 3-2: Use a small aperture or choose landscape mode when photographing landscapes.

Figure 3-3: Use a large aperture or choose portrait mode when photographing a person.

Avoid Lens Distortion

A zoom lens is a wonderful thing. It gives you the creative freedom to compose a scene as you see fit. However, when not used properly, a zoom lens can ruin an otherwise pleasing image. For example, when photographing a building, beginning photographers have a tendency to get as close as possible and then zoom out to get the entire building into the frame. This can lead to distortion, because parallel lines will appear to converge, as shown in Figure 3-4. To avoid distortion, it's best to back away from the building and then zoom in to get the desired composition, as shown in Figure 3-5.

Choose the Right Focal Length

1. Examine the scene through the viewfinder or LCD monitor.

2. As you preview the scene, pay attention to vertical lines. If they appear to be converging in the viewfinder, back away from the scene.

Figure 3-4: Images will be distorted if you select the wrong focal length.

TIP

In low lighting conditions, your camera may have a hard time establishing focus. Aiming a small penlight at your center of interest will help the camera establish focus on that part of the scene.

Figure 3-5: Back away from the scene, and zoom in to capture the image with no distortion.

3. Zoom in to achieve the desired composition.

4. Shoot the picture.

Get a Perfect Exposure Every Time

If you own a high-end digital camera, chances are that you have options to bracket the exposure. Professional photographers bracket an exposure to make sure they'll get the shot. When an exposure is bracketed, three pictures are taken: one with the exposure determined by the camera (Figure 3-6, left), one that is underexposed (Figure 3-6, middle), and one that is overexposed (Figure 3-6, right). When you use auto-exposure bracketing (AEB), you use camera menu options to determine the amount that the images are underexposed and overexposed. Typical settings let you vary the exposure value (EV) from half an f-stop to two f-stops. Your camera menu lets

TIP

If you angle the camera to capture an image of a tall building, your image will be distorted, as the lines at the top of the picture will converge. This distortion can be desirable for artistic images. However, if you want a true rendition of the scene, back up until the entire building is visible in the viewfinder while you're holding the camera parallel to the ground.

Figure 3-6: Bracket the exposure to ensure that you'll get the best shot.

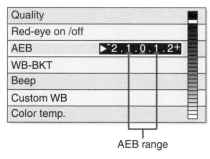

Quality
Red-eye on /off
AEB   ▶⁻2.1.0.1.2⁺
WB-BKT
Beep
Custom WB
Color temp.

AEB range

Figure 3-7: Use camera menu commands to bracket exposures.

you set the exposure bracketing by choosing how much the EV of one image is underexposed and how much the EV of another image is overexposed. The settings for cameras differ. Some cameras have settings that show the number of f-stops. Choosing a setting of 1 changes the EV of the image by one f-stop. Refer to your camera manual for additional information. Auto-exposure bracketing ensures that one of the images will be properly exposed. When you download the images to your computer, you can save the image that suits your needs and discard the others.

Hedge Your Bets with Auto-Exposure Bracketing

1. Access your camera menu.

2. Choose the **Auto-Exposure Bracketing** option. Figure 3-7 shows the auto-exposure bracketing menu for a Canon digital SLR.

3. Set the amount you want the bracketed images to be underexposed and overexposed. Refer to your camera manual for detailed instructions.

4. Close the camera menu, and shoot the desired images.

Figure 3-8: Morning light has subtle pastel shades.

Capture Images in Perfect Light

If you've ever looked at a photograph and been taken in by its beauty, you'll probably notice it has warm tones. Those tones are best captured when you photograph your images in the morning or late afternoon. During the middle of the day, the sun shines down from overhead. The light is direct and harsh, and doesn't cast flattering shadows on the subjects in your scene. Unless you have a reason for including the sun in the picture, shoot with your back to the sun, and try to avoid getting your shadow in the picture.

Shoot Images at the Right Time of Day

1. Shoot images in morning light to get images like Figure 3-8.

2. Shoot images in the late afternoon to get images similar to Figure 3-9.

Figure 3-9: Late afternoon light has warm golden hues.

Take Advantage of Atmospheric Conditions

You can also get wonderful pictures when you might think you'd be better off leaving your camera at home. That is, you can take advantage of the soft diffuse light when it's foggy, misty, or overcast to capture some interesting images, although you'll have to shoot at a higher ISO rating because of the low light. If your camera is capable of shooting close-ups, photograph flowers in the early morning. The dewdrops add compelling highlights to your pictures. If you get a bit of digital noise, it will add to the effect. Just make sure to protect your digital camera when photographing in inclement conditions.

Create Dreamy Images

1. Shoot images in cloudy and overcast conditions to capture images like the one in Figure 3-10.

 **QUICKSTEPS**

CREATING FOG

If you're faced with harsh conditions such as bright noon sun that creates unflattering shadows or the lighting isn't perfect, you can quickly transform conditions by creating fog. If the air is humid enough, simply blow a few breaths onto the glass portion of the camera lens. Wait a second or two for the mist to dissipate, and then take your picture. This technique works with all digital cameras. However, you'll be able to judge exactly how fogged over your lens is if you own a digital SLR or a digital camera that has an electronic through-the-lens viewfinder. If you own a simple point-and-shoot digital camera, breathe on the lens and watch the LCD monitor to determine how misted over the lens is.

Figure 3-10: Cloudy or overcast days create soft, diffuse lighting.

Figure 3-11: Morning dew adds interest to images of flowers.

Figure 3-12: You can use fill flash to brighten shadows.

2. Shoot close-ups of flowers in the early morning to capture images like the one in Figure 3-11. Notice the flower was also photographed with a large lens aperture (a small f-stop number, such as 2.8) so that the background is out of focus.

Master Flash Photography

When you're shooting in total darkness or in dimly lit rooms, you have no other choice but to enable your camera flash. When you photograph with a flash, you often wash out a picture because of the flash's harshness, especially when you're close to your subject. With the exception of photos where detail is lost because you were too close to the subject when the flash went off, you can correct this to some extent by editing the image in an image-editing application. You can also use your camera flash to fill in shadows. For example, if you're photographing someone in a shaded area who has his or her back to the sun, or if your subject is wearing a large hat, fill flash can be used to lighten the shaded areas.

Use Camera Flash

1. Set your camera shooting mode dial to **Automatic**.
2. Press the shutter button halfway. With most cameras, the on-camera flash will pop up in low lighting conditions. You may have to manually engage the flash on your camera. Refer to your manual for further details.
3. Compose and shoot the picture.

Use Fill Flash

1. Switch to one of the creative shooting modes (see Chapter 2).
2. Press your camera flash button to pop up the flash. Most camera flash buttons look like a lightning bolt.
3. Push the shutter button halfway to establish focus. The camera flash will fire a test shot to determine how much light from the flash is needed to properly expose the scene.
4. Press the shutter button fully to take the picture. Figure 3-12 shows an image photographed with fill flash.

PHOTOGRAPHING PEOPLE WITH FLASH

When you photograph a person, pet, or group of people with a flash camera, you may see a condition known as red-eye. This occurs because the subject's pupils are dilated to cope with the dim light. The camera flash bounces off the person's retina back into the camera, making a person's eyes look red and pets' eyes look white. If your camera has a red-eye reduction feature, the camera fires a pre-flash, which causes the subject's pupil to close down and avoid the dilation that causes the red-eye.

DEAL WITH RED-EYE

1. Access your camera menu.

2. Enable red-eye reduction. Refer to your camera manual for the location of your red-eye reduction menu command.

3. Tell the subject to look at the red-eye reduction lamp. Refer to your camera manual for the exact location of this device on your camera.

4. Compose and shoot the picture.

TIP

The red-eye reduction preflash may cause the subject to blink, which means that your subject's eyes may be closed when the main flash goes off. You'll get a more natural picture if you correct the red-eye in an image-editing program such as Adobe Photoshop Elements.

Use Advanced Flash Options

If you own a high-end digital camera or a digital SLR camera, you may have a flash hot shoe: an electrical contact that enables you to connect an external flash to the camera. External flash units are generally more powerful than on-camera flash units. With an external flash unit, you can use what is known as "bounce flash." With bounce flash, the external flash unit is angled toward the ceiling or a wall. The resulting illumination is more diffuse and eliminates harsh shadows in areas such as under the subject's chin. Shadows on the wall are also diffused, resulting in a more pleasing picture. If you use bounce flash, make sure the ceiling or wall off which you bounce the flash is white; otherwise, you'll add a color cast to the image.

Another option for bathing a scene in diffuse light is to attach a piece of white poster board to the flash and swivel the flash upward at a 45 degree angle, as shown here. The flash bounces off the poster board and bathes the subject in diffuse light.

Another option available on many digital cameras is night portrait mode, also called slow-synch flash mode. When you shoot images in this mode, the flash records your subject and the shutter stays open longer to record the background scenery. Many high-end digital cameras and digital SLRs also have an option to fire the flash on second curtain; in other words, just before the shutter closes. This can add interesting effects to images and accentuate motion that occurs prior to the flash firing on the second curtain.

Use Slow-Synch Flash

1. Mount your camera on a tripod. Alternatively, you can take the picture holding the camera, in which case, you'll get a sharp image of your subject, but the background will be soft and somewhat blurry due to camera movement after the flash fires.

2. Switch to one of your camera's creative modes (see Chapter 2).

3. Access your camera menu, and choose the option for slow-synch flash. With some cameras, you may have to choose this option from a camera dial. Refer to your camera manual for further information

4. Enable the camera flash.

5. Compose the picture.

6. Tell your subject to remain perfectly still while the camera records the picture.

7. Press the shutter button halfway. This focuses the scene and causes the flash unit to fire. This initial firing of the flash is used by your camera to compute the amount of light the flash adds to the scene. Your camera may show a message while it computes how long the shutter must remain open to faithfully record the background.

8. Press the shutter button fully to record the image.

Use Second Curtain Shutter

1. Mount your camera on a tripod.

2. Switch to one of your camera's creative modes.

3. Access your camera menu, and choose the option for second curtain shutter.

4. Enable the camera flash.

5. Compose the picture.

6. Press the shutter button halfway. This focuses the scene and causes the flash unit to fire. This initial firing of the flash is used by your camera to compute the amount of light the flash adds to the scene.

7. Press the shutter button fully to capture the image.

Use External Flash

1. Connect your external flash unit to the camera hot shoe.

2. Compose and shoot the picture.

CAUTION

External flash units may take a few seconds to get recharged to full power after you take a picture. If you take another picture before the flash is fully recharged, the picture will be underexposed.

Enhance Your Images with Filters

If your digital camera has threads on the front of the lens mount, you can use photographic filters to enhance your photos. Filters can warm an image, cool it down, tint an image, and so on. The diameter of the threads on the front of your lens determines the size of the filters you can purchase for your camera. A polarizing filter is a handy accessory, which cuts down glare from reflective surfaces like a pool of water. A polarizing filter will also make the sky look bluer. Figure 3-13 (left) shows a scene without a polarizing filter, and Figure 3-13 (right) shows the same scene with a polarizing filter. Notice how the clouds stand out and the sky is bluer in the scene photographed with the polarizing filter. You can find polarizing filters and other popular filters at your local camera store. Table 3-1 lists some of the popular filters and their uses.

Figure 3-13: You can enhance images with the use of filters.

FILTER TYPE	DESCRIPTION
Color-compensating	Warms or cools an image. Warming filters are designated by the numbers 81 and 85, while cooling filters are designated by the numbers 80 and 82. Warming filters add an orange tint to an image, and cooling filters add a blue tint to an image.
Neutral density	Reduces the amount of light reaching the image sensor. Use a neutral-density filter when you want to photograph a scene using a wider aperture (low f-stop number) or a slower shutter speed. Popular neutral-density filters are ND2X (which reduces exposure by one f-stop) and ND4X (which reduces exposure by two f-stops).
Polarizing	Reduces glare from reflective surfaces. Polarizing filters also increase the saturation of the sky, which makes it look bluer and provides good contrast with clouds in the scene.
Skylight	Used to reduce the bluish cast that often appears in images photographed in daylight. This filter adds warmth to an image.
Special effects	A wide variety of special effects filters are available. For example, you can purchase filters that will split a scene into multiple images, add lighting effects such as starbursts, and so on. Visit a camera shop or online camera store to find out more about special effects filters.
Ultraviolet	Filters out ultraviolet rays, which can reduce haze when photographing scenes with distant details. Ultraviolet filters can also be left on a camera lens to protect it against dust and scratches.

Table 3-1: Popular Lens Filters and Their Usage

CAUTION

Do not overtighten or cross-thread a filter when screwing it on a lens.

TIP

You can purchase a filter wrench for most popular filter sizes at a well-stocked camera shop. You use a filter wrench to remove a filter you've inadvertently over-tightened.

Use Filters to Enhance Images

1. Select the desired filter.

2. Gently screw it into the threads on the front of your lens.

3. Compose and shoot the picture.

CREATING HOMEMADE SOFT-FOCUS FILTERS

With a bit of ingenuity, you can create your own filters. For example, to create a soft-focus effect, take a pair of white pantyhose, and cut out a section that's larger than your lens. Cut a small hole in the center of the pantyhose filter. This cut-out area will be in clear focus, while the surrounding image will have a dreamy soft-focus look.

You can also take an inexpensive skylight filter, screw it on the lens mount, and smear the outer perimeter of the filter with a thin film of petroleum jelly. This will also give you a soft-focus effect. Apply more petroleum jelly to the outer perimeter for a graduated transition from clear focus to blurred color. Do not apply any petroleum jelly where you want your subject to be in clear focus. The results of this technique can be seen in the following illustration. If your camera doesn't have a screw-in filter mount, you can place a piece of glass coated with petroleum jelly over the lens. Whichever method you choose, be careful not to get any petroleum jelly on the camera. In fact, it's a good idea to carry a package of moist towelettes in your camera bag to remove any dirt or grime that may have accumulated on your hands before handling your camera.

Use the RAW File Format

Many high-end and most digital SLRs have the capability to capture images in the RAW format. A RAW image is pure digital data—exactly what the image sensor recorded. The image is not processed; therefore, no compression is applied to the image and you have more data with which to work. Many beginning photographers shy away from capturing in RAW format, because it takes up a lot of room on the memory card and most camera manuals don't give clear-cut instructions on how to work with RAW images after capturing them. After you download the image to your computer, you can view it using the viewer supplied by the camera manufacturer. You can then correct for any deficiencies in exposure, correct white balance, sharpen the image, control image contrast and saturation, and so on. After processing the image, save it as a JPEG or TIFF file. Processing images captured in RAW format will be covered in Chapter 7.

Capture Images Using the RAW Format

When you capture images in RAW mode, you'll have to switch to one of the creative modes: aperture mode, shutter mode, or manual mode. Some cameras offer a program mode as well. When you capture an image in RAW mode, your camera creates two files: the image and a thumbnail of the image. Your camera may also have the option to capture images in the RAW and JPEG formats at the same time.

1. Turn the camera mode dial to select the desired creative shooting mode.
2. From the camera menu image size section, choose the **RAW** format.
3. Capture the image.
4. Download the image to your computer.

5. View the image on the associated viewer. Figure 3-14 shows a RAW file as viewed in the Photoshop Elements 5 Camera Raw plug-in.

6. Export the image in the desired file format for further processing.

Figure 3-14: Process RAW images and then save them using the desired file format.

Chapter 4

Shooting Landscapes, Animals, People, and Objects

After you learn the basic functions of your digital camera, you're ready to capture digital images of your world. You can use your digital camera to take compelling pictures of landscapes, friends, and loved ones. In this chapter you'll learn techniques to photograph landscapes, people, animals, and objects.

Capture Your World Digitally

A digital camera is a wonderful thing. You can carry it with you wherever you go and capture images of the moments, places, and people that are important in your life. Time is a fleeting thing, and some events can never be recaptured, but after you click the shutter on your digital camera, you know within a second or so whether you have a compelling picture of the moment or not. In the upcoming sections, you'll learn some techniques that will help you digitally capture the special times in your life.

Photograph Landscapes

Photographing landscapes requires developing an eye for recognizing interesting scenes and then creating a dramatic composition. You don't have to be in a hurry when photographing a landscape, but you do need to plan your photograph. First and foremost, photograph the landscape during the golden light of the morning or late afternoon. Other than the time of day, you can take your time, as landscapes are static and do not change, unless, of course, you want to capture atmospheric phenomena, such as a brewing thunderstorm.

Photograph Scenic Vistas

When you photograph a landscape, examine the vista from all angles. Look for an interesting composition that draws your viewer into the scene. If you're serious about photographing landscapes, study the work of master landscape photographers, like Ansel Adams.

1. Choose the proper composition. If you're photographing a landscape with rolling mountains or hills, a horizontal composition works best, as shown here:

2. If you're photographing a landscape with a tall feature, such as a towering sequoia or a waterfall, a vertical composition and low camera angle will accentuate the feature, as shown in the image to the left.

3. Position the horizon. Many beginning photographers place the horizon in the middle of the picture, but you can add a sense of grandeur to a scene when you lower the horizon line, as shown below.

4. Shoot the scene with the smallest possible aperture (a large f-stop number) for the maximum depth of field. If you're shooting the scene with a point-and-shoot digital camera, choose the landscape shooting mode. Record the scene using aperture priority mode if your camera is so equipped, and choose an f-stop of f/11 or greater. (See Chapter 2 for more information.) If you're shooting in dim lighting conditions, you may have to increase the ISO rating in order to achieve a fast enough shutter speed.

5. Zoom to achieve the desired composition. As a rule, when you shoot a landscape, you shoot with a wide angle lens. A lens with a 35-mm equivalent of 28 mm will give you pleasing results. If you're capturing a majestic landscape, you can shoot using a lens with a 35-mm equivalent of 20 mm or less. The following image is a sunset seascape photographed with an ultra-wide angle lens.

TIP

If possible, when composing a landscape scene, include objects near the camera, such as blades of tall grass or flowers. Shoot the scene with the smallest possible aperture, as outlined in step 4, and all elements in the scene will be in sharp focus.

TIP

If you own a polarizing filter, use it to increase contrast when photographing skyscapes. Twist the outer ring of the polarizing filter to deepen the blues in the sky. You'll notice the most difference when the sun is at a 90-degree angle to the subject you are photographing.

6. Take several photographs of the scene from different vantage points and camera angles. Remember, if you don't like an image, you can always delete it.

Photograph Skyscapes

You can also create dramatic photographs of cloud formations. When photographing a skyscape, the sky should be the predominant object in your photograph. You'll get the best photographs of clouds if you photograph early in the morning or late in the afternoon or around sunset. Additional tips include the following:

- Zoom in directly on the cloud formation, and include no landscape elements in the picture.

  –Or–

- Photograph an interesting cloud formation at sunrise or sunset, with a non-distracting foreground, as shown in the illustration to the left.

Photograph Oceans, Lakes, and Waterfalls

Man has always been lured to the water. The sound of waves crashing against the shore or a babbling brook are hypnotic and soothing. You can capture the tranquility and beauty of oceans, lakes, and waterfalls with your digital camera.

Photograph Seascapes

1. When you photograph a seascape, shoot with a wide-angle lens to capture the vastness of the ocean, and include other features to tie the viewer to a geographical location. Another option is to create a dramatic picture by zooming in and capturing a wave crashing into the shore. Zoom out to capture the expanse of a seascape. Include geographical features, such as in the image to the left, which shows the towering cliffs at Drakes Beach in California.

2. Zoom In on a wave, and shoot with a high shutter speed to create a wavescape, as shown in the following photograph.

PHOTOGRAPHING CITYSCAPES

Big cities are exciting places to visit—and to photograph. Most major metropolitan areas have distinguishing landmarks. New York City has the Empire State Building, San Francisco has the Transamerica Building, and St. Louis has its trademark arch. Photos of a famous landmark instantly trigger memories of your visit.

1. Photographing a cityscape is just like photographing a vast landscape of plains and mountains. Set your camera to landscape mode. Or, if you can manually adjust the camera, choose aperture priority mode and the smallest aperture (large f-stop number) possible while still maintaining a high-enough shutter speed to avoid blurring. Compose a view of the skyline of the city you are visiting, but try to avoid the cliché shot that appears in every tourist brochure. If you live in the city, you'll know just which shots to avoid.

2. If you're photographing a skyline, choose a horizontal composition, as shown in the illustration. Notice how the curved seawall leads your eye to the drawbridge and then to the skyline of Tampa, Florida.

Continued . . .

Photograph Lakes

Lakes can make interesting subjects for photos. The key to creating a good photograph of a lake is lighting. Your photos will be enhanced if you have interesting clouds or other subjects in the scene to direct the viewer's eye. A dock or boat is a useful object to draw your viewer into a scene. Or you can include a natural object associated with a region, such as the hanging Spanish moss, as shown in the photograph of a sunset on a Florida lake.

Photograph Brooks and Waterfalls

When you photograph waves, you use a high shutter speed to freeze the wave. You can also use a high shutter speed to stop the motion of a brook or waterfall. However, you can also use a slow shutter speed to capture an image of a brook or waterfall, which will create graceful

PHOTOGRAPHING CITYSCAPES *(Continued)*

3. If a tall landmark appears in your scene, consider a vertical composition. The image to the right shows the famous minarets of the University of Tampa in Tampa, Florida.

4. To create a slice of life, photograph a busy city street, and use a zoom lens at a high level of magnification. The following image depicts Stockton Street in San Francisco's Chinatown. Notice how the high degree of magnification makes the buildings appear to be closer together than they actually are.

patterns of flowing water, as shown in the following image.

Take Your Digital Camera on the Road

Digital photography can be downright addictive. With no film to buy and no film to process, there's no reason your digital camera shouldn't be a constant companion. You never know when a photo opportunity will present itself. Of course, you should always take your digital camera when you go on vacation. Vacations are special times with friends and family that fade quickly from memory once you're back into your daily routine. However, you can relive your vacation at any time by reviewing your digital journal of the trip.

QUICKFACTS

PHOTOGRAPHING SCENES AT SUNRISE AND SUNSET

Whether you capture a sunrise or sunset will depend on the area in which you live, the geographical features you want to include in your picture, and your own internal clock. If you want mountains in your picture and the mountains lie to your east, you photograph at sunrise. If you want the ocean in your picture and the ocean is to your west, you photograph at sunset. If you're a morning person, you photograph a scene that looks good at sunrise; if you're a night owl, you photograph a scene that looks good at sunset. When photographing sunrises and sunsets, your camera may have a tendency to underexpose the scene to compensate for the brightness of the sun. Your camera may have a mode for shooting sunrises and sunsets that will expose the scene correctly. If not, overexpose the scene by one or two f-stops to maintain detail. If your camera has a tendency to create a bright halo when shooting directly into the sun, hide the sun behind a tree or building, as shown in the photograph here.

CAUTION

Never look directly at the sun through the viewfinder, as it may damage your vision.

Plan Before Your Vacation

1. Research your trip ahead of time:

   - Review Web sites for the cities you intend to visit, and note any places of interest you would like to photograph.
   - Review travel brochures to see how other photographers have photographed the area you intend to visit.
   - Review the Web sites of professional photographers in the area you're going to visit. You can often find compelling photos of the area that will give you ideas for your own photos.

2. Pack your camera gear:

   - Be sure you have extra memory cards or a laptop computer to which you can download your images.
   - Pack extra batteries.

   - Remember to pack your battery charger. If you're traveling overseas, make sure your battery charger will work in the countries you are visiting. Otherwise, purchase a voltage adapter. When you purchase a power adapter, make sure it's the same voltage and frequency as that of the country you're visiting.
   - Pack your camera lens cleaning equipment.
   - If desired, pack a tripod. Note that you can purchase lightweight tripods that can be packed in luggage. You may be charged a fee when using a tripod on certain historical sites. Check with the country you are visiting or your travel agent for more details.
   - Pack your camera gear in your carry-on luggage; otherwise, rough baggage handlers may damage your camera. And there's always the possibility that your camera may get stolen by a less-than-honest baggage handler or security person.

QUICK**FACTS**

GOING BEYOND THE PERFECT SUNRISE AND SUNSET

Many people believe that once the sun goes down, the sunset is over. When you photograph a beautiful sunset with billowing clouds, wait a few minutes. Even though the sun is below the horizon, it still illuminates the clouds. Wait for 10 or 15 minutes, and you'll see the clouds become transformed with shades of pink and purple. At sunrise, the opposite happens. A few minutes before sunrise, the clouds are bathed with subtle pastel hues of pink and blue. When you photograph scenes before sunrise and after sunset, you may find that automatic exposure will make the image brighter than the actual scene. You'll notice this in your LCD monitor after your camera captures the picture. When this happens, use your camera menu command or control to reduce the exposure by an f-stop. The image here shows a scene photographed several minutes after sunset.

TIP

When you travel, use a nondescript case to house your camera gear. An expensive camera case with a manufacturer's logo is like sending a written invitation to a thief. Never leave your camera gear unattended. A diaper bag is a good alternative.

Photograph Your Vacation

1. Photograph subjects or buildings that people will associate with the places you visit. Remember to examine the scene and photograph it from a unique vantage point to add your own creative touch to the photos. For example, the image shows the Washington Monument photographed from the Vietnam War Memorial.

2. Include pictures of friends or relatives in front of historical landmarks or other scenic vistas. If you can, photograph people with their backs to the sun to avoid squinting faces, and remember to compensate for backlit subjects. Compose pictures of this type so that the people in the picture and the landmark are identifiable. Avoid mistakes like having the Leaning Tower of Pisa growing out of someone's head.

3. To include yourself in pictures with friends and relatives, ask a passerby who looks trustworthy to take the picture. Compose the scene first and then hand the camera to the passerby and instruct him or her on how to release the shutter.

4. Capture the special moments. For example, if your vacation involves air flight, take a picture of a loved one catching a catnap before boarding a flight.

5. Try to plan visits to major tourist attractions on off days. This helps you avoid fighting long lines and crowds of people. As an added benefit, you get pictures of the tourist attraction without massive throngs of tourists in every shot.

6. If you're staying in the same city for several days, photograph historical landmarks or unique vistas at different times of the day and in different weather conditions. Clouds and the setting sun can add ambiance to what would otherwise be a bland photo.

7. Make your visit coincide with any interesting parades or activities that take place in the city you plan to visit. You can generally find this type of information on the city's Web site. Arrive at the event early so that you can claim a good spot on the sidelines. This will enable you to photograph the event without including other spectators.

Photograph People in Public Places

When you travel to a distant locale, people pictures help document your visit. For example, a visit to San Francisco's Chinatown would not be complete without capturing images of the Chinese men and women playing mah jong in Portsmouth Square. However, most people shy away from having their pictures taken by strangers. Here are a few techniques you can use to catch spontaneous pictures of people:

- Photograph the scene from a distance using a zoom lens, as shown in the illustration to the right.

TIP

Some people do not want their photographs taken. If someone asks you to delete the picture, delete it. Also, there are several laws regarding privacy. Be sure you're not violating a person's privacy when taking their picture.

TIP

When photographing a group of people inside a building, take some photos from the second-floor balcony, if the building has one. Your subjects won't be aware of your camera and you'll get more natural-looking pictures. Of course, you can always spice things up by calling someone's name and then taking the picture as that person looks up at you.

TIP

If your camera has an option to capture images continually after you press the shutter button, you can capture several photos from a scene, such as a bride and groom's first kiss after sealing their vows.

- If you own a camera with an LCD viewer, sit at a nearby table, open the LCD viewer, and compose the scene. People won't think you're taking their picture if you're not looking at them through the main viewfinder.
- Do not use the camera flash, as this is a dead giveaway you're taking a picture.

Photograph Friends and Family

A digital camera is a wonderful way to capture the special moments and times of the important people in your life. Many people adopt an unnatural pose when a camera is pointed at them, while others are just natural hams in front of the camera. Knowing your subject is the key to getting a good picture. If your subject is uncomfortable in front of the camera, back up a bit and give some room. Keep your finger poised on the shutter button, and click it when you see something you like. And if someone asks you not to take their picture, respect the person and do as they request.

Capture Digital Images of Friends and Family

1. Compose your picture, remembering to place the main subject at a point of interest. For more information on composing images, refer to Chapter 3.

2. Choose an interesting vantage point. For example, when photographing a young child, position the child on a chair so that you're photographing from the same level or slightly lower than the child.

3. Avoid taking photographs of people when they're eating.

4. When photographing an event, such as a wedding or birthday, take several shots to capture the range of emotions.

5. When at an informal event, such as a party, keep on the move and take photos from several vantage points.

6. Avoid distracting backgrounds. Your friends and family are the stars of your images.

7. When taking a picture of two people, zoom in tight and compose the picture so that the subjects' heads are aligned with points of interest (the Rule of Thirds).

Capture a Digital Portrait

1. Step away from the subject.

2. Rotate the camera 90 degrees, and frame the subject vertically.

3. Zoom in to achieve the desired composition. You can zoom in for a head-and-shoulders portrait, as shown, or zoom in tight and capture just the person's face and part of the hair. The latter is known as an extreme close-up.

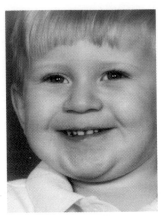

4. Talk to your subject to relax him or her while you're photographing. Ask questions about likes and dislikes, family members, or hobbies. A relaxed subject will give you more natural pictures.

5. Make sure the subject's eyes are in focus. Remember, the eyes are the windows to the soul. If possible, compose the photograph so that one of the subject's eyes intersects a point of interest (the Rule of Thirds), as shown in this photograph (right).

Photograph a Group of People

1. Find a unique vantage point from which to photograph your scene. For example, when you photograph a group of people at a table, avoid the head-on shot from the end of the table. If you stand on top of a chair or on the second or third rung of a stepladder and photograph the group from above, you'll create a more interesting photo.

2. Take control of the situation, and tell your subjects where you want them to stand. If you're photographing a large group of people, tell the taller people to move to the back, and position small children in the front of the photo. You can also ask the first row of people to kneel.

TIP

You'll get more pleasing portraits if you use available light instead of relying on the camera flash. Photograph your subject seated in a chair staring out a window on a cloudy day. The soft light won't create any harsh shadows and helps hide unwanted facial features, such as wrinkles and crow's feet.

TIP

If you must use a flash when shooting a portrait, put a piece of tissue paper or a small square cut out of a plastic milk carton in front of the flash. This will diffuse the light, resulting in a more flattering portrait.

TIP

If you're photographing a really large group, take the pictures outdoors, if possible.

QUICKSTEPS

TAKING A DIGITAL SELF-PORTRAIT

If your camera is equipped with a self-timer, you can take a picture of yourself. Your camera's self-timer may be menu-driven, although some cameras have external controls for this feature. The self-timer counts down a given interval before taking the picture. This gives you time to move into the frame. Some cameras have two self-timer time selections: generally two to five seconds and ten seconds. The self-timer can also be used to include you in a photograph with friends or family.

1. Position your camera on a tripod.

2. Enable the self-timer feature.

3. Compose the picture.

4. Press the shutter button.

5. Walk into the frame, and wait until the shutter opens and closes. Most cameras with a self-timer feature will flash a light as the camera counts down. The flashes become more rapid just before the shutter opens, which is your cue to smile for the camera.

6. If your camera is capable of long exposures, move to one position and stand still for a few seconds, then move to another position, and so on. The image to the right shows two ghostlike images of the author in front of a sculpture in Tampa.

TIP

If you don't have a tripod, place your camera on something soft, like a folded-up sweater or jacket.

3. As you compose the scene through the viewfinder, be aware of any gaps between people. Also make sure that all of your subjects are visible in the viewfinder. It's okay to crop off part of a subject's arm, but avoid cropping off someone's facial features. If necessary, back up a little.

4. Tell your group to strike different poses to avoid the "police lineup" syndrome, where everyone is ramrod-straight and their gaze is fixed on the photographer.

5. Take several photos to make sure you catch everyone looking their best. Remember, you can always delete the bloopers where some of your subjects had their eyes closed or were in mid-yawn when you snapped the picture.

Photograph Nature

If you live near a wildlife reserve or a remote lake, you can use your digital camera to capture wonderful images of nature. You can also capture images of wildlife at your local zoo. Each type of photography is equally challenging, and you'll face some obstacles when trying to capture the perfect image. When photographing wildlife, use a bit of common sense and keep your distance. Rely on your camera zoom lens to get close-ups. Even the most docile animals will attack if they feel threatened or provoked. Shooting wildlife with a camera can be rewarding. This is a different type of hunting, where you end up with a trophy picture instead of depleting the population of the species.

Photograph Wildlife and Nature

1. If you're photographing animals like bears or deer, stay downwind of the animals so that your scent won't give you away.

2. If possible, photograph the animal from higher ground.

CAPTURING IMAGES OF THE FAMILY'S BEST FRIEND

Dogs and cats are treasured family members and can be wonderful subjects for your digital photographs. Dogs and cats have totally different personalities. Dogs are content to follow their masters everywhere, whereas cats can be somewhat aloof. Big dogs can be the subjects of wonderful action shots as they jump high to catch a Frisbee. A cat will strike a contemplative Zen-like pose as it gazes into the distance for minutes at a time—that is, until you grab a string and dangle it in front of the cat's face. Avoid photographing your pets with flash. First, they don't like the bright light and will shy away from you the next time you point a camera in their direction. Second, dogs and cats are also subject to red-eye, but in the case of dogs and cats, the reflection from the animal's retina makes your pet's eyes look like they're glowing.

1. Photograph large dogs against a plain background. If you photograph a large dog with black fur against a dark background, the animal will be lost in the picture.

2. If you're photographing a pet with dark fur, photograph the animal against a light background.

3. Take photos of your cat staring out the window. The soft diffuse lighting will highlight the animal's fur and provide wonderful catch-lights in the cat's eyes.

4. Zoom in on your pet, and choose the largest possible aperture (small f-stop number) to blur the background.

5. Point your camera at your pet and call your pet's name while she's napping. Snap the picture when she perks up her ears and looks at you.

3. Switch to aperture priority mode if your camera has it, and choose a large aperture (low f-stop number). If you own a point-and-shoot digital camera, switch to portrait mode. Either method will create a blurry foreground and background, with the animal you are photographing in sharp focus, as shown. Alternatively, if you're photographing rapidly moving animals, switch to shutter priority mode and choose a shutter speed fast enough (1/500 of a second or faster) to freeze the animal in motion.

4. Zoom in on the animal and compose the scene.

5. Shoot the picture.

Capture Images in a Zoo

With a bit of planning and persistence, you can take pictures of animals at a zoo that look like they were taken in the wild. You do face obstacles when you photograph at a zoo, however. For one, there is the fencing that keeps the wildlife within the zoo. You also have other spectators viewing the animals. To capture realistic wildlife images from a zoo, you'll have to minimize both obstacles.

1. If possible, plan your visit to the zoo on a weekday to minimize the amount of spectators you'll have to work around, especially if you're visiting a famous zoo, like the San Diego Zoo.

2. Choose a vantage point with a natural background. If possible, shoot from a high vantage point. This will enable you to shoot over fences.

3. If you're forced to photograph through a chain-link fence, zoom in or use a telephoto lens. Switch to aperture priority mode, and choose a large aperture (low f-stop number), which will throw the chain-link fence out of focus and make it less apparent. When shooting through a fence, you'll also have to manually focus on the animal. Otherwise, the camera will focus on the fencing, as it is the nearest thing to the camera.

4. Zoom in on the animal.

5. Compose and shoot the picture.

Photograph Birds

You can create dramatic pictures of nesting birds and birds in flight with your digital camera. You can capture pictures of birds in your own backyard, if you have a bird feeder, or you can photograph them at a local lake.

1. To photograph stationary birds, choose aperture priority mode, and then choose a large aperture (small f-stop number). If your camera doesn't have an aperture priority mode, choose portrait mode. This throws the background out of focus, which makes sure your viewer's eye is drawn to the bird.

2. To photograph birds in flight, switch to shutter priority mode, and then choose a shutter speed of 1/500 of a second or higher to capture an image similar to the one shown. If your camera isn't equipped with a shutter priority mode, choose sports mode.

3. Zoom in on the bird.

4. Shoot the picture.

Take Photographs for eBay Auctions

A picture is worth a thousand words, even more so when you're trying to sell something. eBay is the source many people turn to when they need to sell items they no longer use, such as items that have been replaced with newer technology, jewelry, and just about any other imaginable item. The biggest problem with most auctions is the photos, especially when the photos are of small items. The photos are often blurry, lack detail, and have dark shadows.

Photograph Objects for eBay Auctions

When you decide to take photos of an item for eBay auctions, lighting and the clarity or sharpness of the image are two important factors. Here are a few steps you can take that will increase your chances of capturing good photos of items you want to auction on eBay.

1. Switch to macro mode when photographing small items. If you own a digital SLR, you can either purchase a macro lens or macro attachments for your normal lens.

2. Shoot the pictures in aperture priority mode, and choose a small aperture (high f-stop number) to ensure that the entire item is in focus.

3. Use a plain backdrop for the picture. In a pinch, white sheets work well. Another alternative is to place the object on a white piece of foam core, and use another piece of foam core for the backdrop.

4. Do not use the on-camera flash, especially on shiny objects. If you have an external flash, bounce it off a white piece of foam core. This will give you soft diffuse lighting with soft shadows. If you don't have an external flash, place a piece of white fabric over the flash to diffuse the harsh light.

5. Another option is natural light. Photograph the object outdoors on an overcast day or in even shade, which is an area that's completely shaded with no sunlight filtering in. You can also use window light to photograph the object. If you use window light, place a piece of foam core or a white sheet on the shadow side of the object to bounce light into the shadows.

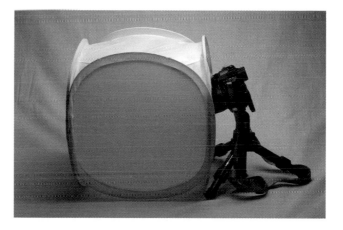

6. Mount your camera on a tripod. This will ensure that the picture is sharp.

7. Zoom in so that the subject fills the frame. If you have a lot of white space around the object, it will be hard to spot when reduced to the size at which it will be displayed in your eBay listing.

8. Turn the camera vertically when photographing objects that are taller than they are wide.

9. If you sell a lot of items on eBay, purchase a cube soft box, such as the one shown. Place the object you want to photograph inside the cube, and place a light overhead, or place a light on each side of the cube. You can also use the cube soft box outside on a bright sunny day. The fabric diffuses the light, producing a soft, shadow-free light that is perfect for photographing objects. Most cube soft boxes come with different backgrounds. Many eBay vendors sell these devices. On eBay's home page, search for "cube soft box" or "tent soft box." Prices vary, depending on the size you purchase. Figure 4-1 shows an object that was photographed with a cube soft box.

Figure 4-1: Cube soft boxes are ideal for photographing objects for eBay auctions.

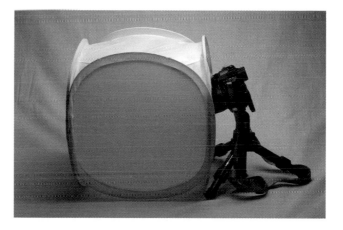

TIP

If you have your own Web site, post larger versions of the photos there and include links in your listing that, when clicked, will display the larger image.

Chapter 5
Shooting Action Sequences

When you take a photo of a person or landscape, you have a static subject, and lighting and composition become your main concerns. However, when you want to use your digital camera to take pictures of people or objects in motion, you have different challenges. In addition to dealing with lighting and composition, you have to portray motion in your images. In this chapter, you'll learn several techniques for capturing motion with your digital camera.

Capture Action with Your Digital Camera

It would be wonderful if you could freeze time for a brief second to capture a moving object with your digital camera and then, with a snap of the fingers, resume time. In essence, that's what your finished image is in most cases—a

Figure 5-1: **You can capture action by choosing the right settings on your digital camera.**

slice of time where you've captured the essence of motion, be it an athlete caught in mid-flight while vaulting the pole in a high jump or a batter in mid-swing. If you've used a film camera to photograph action, you may think you can use the same techniques, and you're almost right. Digital cameras are close to their film-bearing brethren, but digital cameras have to "think" after you press the shutter button. Therefore, you have to think ahead in order to capture a wonderful action scene, such as the one shown in Figure 5-1, instead of a blurry, unrecognizable image.

Deal with Shutter Lag

Most of the newer high-end digital cameras and digital SLRs have negligible shutter lag. However, if you own a less expensive point-and-shoot digital camera, you may still experience shutter lag in certain conditions, such as when you're capturing images of moving objects. Shutter lag is the amount of time between when you press the shutter button and when the camera actually captures the picture. The reasons for this are the myriad functions the camera performs after you press the shutter. The camera focuses on the subject and then replaces the current contents of the image sensor (the last picture you took) with the subject you are photographing. If you notice that your camera exhibits shutter lag that is noticeable, here are some ways you can overcome it:

- Press the shutter button halfway to pre-focus on an object that is equidistant from the camera to the area where you will photograph your subject in motion. Alternatively, you can switch to landscape or infinity mode, which increases the depth of field. If you enable landscape mode, your camera may revert to a slow shutter speed. If this is the case, you'll have to pan the camera with the subject, as outlined in "Pan the Camera." Another alternative is to use your camera's manual focus mode to focus on the area where your subject will appear.

- Anticipate the shutter lag and press the shutter button an instant before the action you want to capture comes into frame.

Practice taking pictures of different moving subjects in various lighting conditions. Choose the largest image size and highest quality your camera has available, unless your camera has excessive shutter lag. If this is the case, choose an image size and quality that will enable you to quickly capture the action and still create an acceptable image. If your goal is to freeze motion, choose a shutter speed that is fast enough to freeze motion. The shutter speed will vary, depending on how fast the subject is moving. If you're photographing a runner, you can use a shutter speed of 1/125 of a second. If you're photographing a race car rounding a corner and your goal is to freeze the action, a good starting point is 1/2000 of a second. As you press the shutter, make a mental note of the amount of shutter lag in different picture-taking conditions. This will help you anticipate when you need to press the shutter button to thwart shutter lag as a subject moves into view.

Figure 5-2: Pan the camera to capture images of objects in motion.

- Reduce to a lower image quality, unless you're going to print your images. It takes your camera longer to record a large image with the highest quality. Therefore, a lower image quality will reduce the amount of time it takes your camera to process images and enable you to take additional photos quicker once the camera buffer is full.

- Enable your camera's continuous focus mode, if it's so equipped. In this mode, the camera continually focuses on an object moving toward or away from you.

- Enable your camera's continuous shooting or burst mode. This mode enables you to snap a series of pictures as long as the shutter button is held down. The images are stored in the camera memory buffer and then transferred to your removable storage media. Once the buffer is full, you will have to wait for it to empty before you can continue taking pictures. Cameras with continuous or burst mode are capable of capturing three to nine images per second, depending on the camera manufacturer and model.

- Make sure your camera is not in standby mode when the action is fast and furious, as it may take your camera a second or two to wake up when you press the shutter button.

Pan the Camera

If you shoot with a high-enough shutter speed, you can freeze action. However, there are times when you need to track a subject before taking the picture. For example, if you're photographing a bird in flight, you synchronize the motion of the camera with that of the bird in flight and then snap the picture at the desired moment, as shown in Figure 5-2.

1. Switch to continuous focus mode, if your camera is equipped with this feature. If not, switch your camera to landscape or infinity mode.

2. Plant your feet firmly, align the moving subject in your viewfinder, and zoom in to the desired degree of magnification.

3. Press the shutter button halfway to establish focus.

4. As the subject moves toward you, twist your torso so that your moving subject remains centered in your viewfinder. As the subject comes closer, you'll have to move faster to keep the subject in frame.

5. Press the shutter button when the subject is at the desired point.

Create a Sequence of Images

When you want to capture a sequence of images, such as a tennis player serving or returning a volley, you can use your camera's burst or continuous mode. When you shoot in burst mode, the camera continues recording images as long as you hold down the shutter button or until your camera memory buffer is full. Shooting a sequence of images is a wonderful way to record an exciting action sequence.

1. Choose the menu item or press the button on your camera that enables continuous or burst shooting mode.

2. Switch to continuous focus mode, if your camera is so equipped.

3. Press the shutter button halfway to focus on the subject.

4. Press the shutter button fully, and hold it down to create a sequence of images, as shown in Figure 5-3. To capture the essence of speed, a slow shutter speed was selected, and the camera was panned with the cyclist, which created the blurry background.

Capture the Essence of Motion

Images of athletes and animals in motion depict grace, agility, and power. When you see images of animals in motion with details such as sinewy muscles and rippling fur, it's almost like being there. There are a couple of ways you can create compelling pictures of objects in motion with your digital camera—the actual method you use depends on your subject. When you're photographing a subject such as a pole vaulter springing over the high bar, you can freeze the action, because it's readily apparent your subject is in motion. However, when you photograph an object like a race car, traveling at well over 100 mph, freezing the action makes it look like you snapped a picture of a car parked on the track. Your goal in this instance is to capture all of the detail on the car and still convey the sense of speed. The next two sections show you how to photograph both types of objects.

*Figure 5-3: **Capture motion with a sequence of images.***

TIP

If your camera does not have continuous focus mode and the subject is moving toward you, choose landscape or infinity mode to assure the greatest depth of field.

QUICKFACTS

STEADYING THE CAMERA

When you're working with a zoom lens at extreme magnification or a high-powered telephoto lens, the slightest camera shake is magnified and can result in an unclear picture. You also run the risk of a blurry image when you photograph with a slow shutter speed. A tripod is the ideal solution for steadying a camera. However, tripods are cumbersome and can limit your mobility, especially when you need to be mobile to capture the action. With a bit of practice, you can learn to steady the camera and get sharper pictures. To do this, plant your feet firmly, with one foot slightly in front of the other. Your feet should also be spread slightly apart, similar to the legs on a tripod. Cradle the underside of the camera lens with one hand, and firmly grasp the camera body with the other. Position your arms close to the sides of your chest. Before taking the picture, inhale and then slowly squeeze the shutter button while remaining still. If you're shooting a vertical composition, plant your feet firmly and steady the camera by placing one arm close to your chest, as shown here.

Photograph Rapidly Moving Subjects

When you photograph a subject such as a downhill skier or a pitcher unleashing a blazing fastball, your goal is to freeze the motion. A photograph of a skier with flakes of snow flying from the tips of his skis makes it readily apparent that the skier is traveling rapidly.

1. If you're using a point-and-shoot camera, switch to sports mode.
2. If you're using a high-end digital camera or digital SLR, switch to shutter priority mode, and choose a shutter speed of 1/1000 of a second or more. You may have to increase the ISO rating to achieve a shutter speed that is fast enough to freeze the action.
3. Switch to continuous focus mode, if your camera is so equipped.
4. If the subject is traveling toward you, press the shutter button halfway to establish focus. If your camera is not equipped with a continuous focus mode, pre-focus on an object equidistant to the place where your subject will be when you capture the image.
5. Press the shutter button fully to capture the desired image.

Blur Image Backgrounds to Enhance Motion

When photographing rapidly moving vehicles, the practice of using a high shutter speed goes right out the window. Sure, you freeze the action, but you also freeze everything else, including the rapidly rotating wheels and tires. The image you end up with looks like you took a picture of a parked vehicle. The solution is to use a slow shutter speed and pan with the subject.

1. Switch to shutter priority mode.
2. Choose a slow shutter speed of 1/125 of a second when photographing objects like race cars. If you're photographing slower vehicles, like racing bicycles, you can use a shutter speed as low as 1/60 of a second.
3. Pre-focus the camera on a subject that is equidistant to the point at which you will take the picture, or choose continuous focus mode, if your camera has this feature.

Synchronizing your camera with a moving subject takes practice. Begin by panning your camera with slower-moving objects, such as children on bicycles, and then move up to faster-moving objects, such as speeding cars or birds in flight. With a bit of practice, panning will become second nature.

Continue panning after you press the shutter button to ensure that the subject's motion is still synchronized with that of the camera. If you stop panning at the instant you press the shutter button, your subject will not be sharp, because it is still moving but your camera is not. This is especially important if you're photographing fast-moving objects at slower shutter speeds.

If your camera takes a second or two to power up, when photographing action or a sporting event, use your camera menu to increase the amount of time before your camera goes into standby mode. This will shorten battery life, but your camera will be at the ready when you press the shutter button. After photographing the action, you can decrease the amount of time before your camera goes into standby mode to conserve battery life.

4. When the vehicle comes into view, center it in your viewfinder, and begin panning the camera with the vehicle, as outlined previously. Pan smoothly, synchronizing the motion of the camera with the moving object.

5. Press the shutter button fully when the vehicle reaches the desired position. Remember to continue panning after you press the shutter button. An image taken using this technique is shown here.

Photograph a Sporting Event

You can capture wonderful images of sporting events with your digital camera. For example, if one of your children is on a school team, you can capture one of the team's events for posterity. When you photograph a local sporting event, you usually don't have to contend with huge crowds. You may be able to get unlimited access, which enables you to take photographs from many different vantage points. And that's the key to capturing good images at a sporting event: take a wide variety of pictures from different vantage points.

QUICKSTEPS

STEADYING YOUR CAMERA WITH A MONOPOD

You can also use a monopod to steady a camera. A monopod is a lightweight alternative to a tripod. This device is similar to a walking cane and, as the name implies, has one (mono) leg (pod) and a mounting screw you attach to your camera's tripod mount. A monopod has a series of interlocking tubes that you extend or retract to adjust the device to the desired height. Many monopods also feature a retractable three-legged foot that can be accessed by unscrewing the mount at the bottom of the tripod.

1. Connect the monopod to the bottom of your camera.

2. Loosen the locking collars, extend the monopod to the desired height, and then tighten the locking collars.

3. Extract the monopod's retractable foot, if so equipped.

4. Plant your feet firmly and cradle the camera, as outlined in the QuickFacts "Steadying the Camera." In essence, your two feet form the second and third legs of a tripod when used in conjunction with a monopod.

5. Compose your picture and then press the shutter button halfway to focus on your subject.

6. Inhale and then slowly press the shutter button fully to take the picture, as shown in the illustration.

Another possibility is photographing a major sporting event, such as a professional football game or an automobile race. When you photograph a major sporting event, you will have to contend with crowds, and you won't be given carte blanche access to certain places. However, with a bit of planning and creative thinking, you'll be able to take memorable pictures. The upcoming sections describe a few techniques you can use to photograph local and major sporting events with your digital camera. When you photograph a sporting event, you're telling a story. Photograph all stages of the event, from beginning to conclusion. You can also capture compelling images of the athletes' awards ceremony or victory celebration.

Take Photographs Before a Sporting Event

When athletes prepare for competition, they perform time-honored rituals. For example, marathon runners stretch and then loosen up by jogging. At an automobile race, race cars are prepared in the paddock, while the drivers prepare their equipment and don fireproof clothing. Capture photos of the drivers in their cars as they drive out of the pits to the starting grid, as shown in Figure 5-4. When you capture behind-the-scenes images, you capture more of the ambience of the event, rather than the typical cut-and-dried static photos taken by noncreative photographers.

1. Arrive at the event early.

2. If you're photographing a local event, such as a high school football game, ask for permission to photograph the athletes as they prepare for the event. You can capture some wonderful images of athletes adjusting shoulder pads and strapping on kneepads, helmets, and so on. Another possibility is a close-up of an athlete's eyes as photographed through a helmet.

3. When photographing close-up images of athletes, switch to portrait mode. Alternatively, switch to aperture priority mode, if your camera is so equipped, and shoot with the largest possible aperture (small f-stop number) to create a limited depth of field. Your goal is a crisp picture where the athlete is in sharp focus but the background is blurred.

TIP

When using a monopod to steady the camera while photographing in a low-light situation, switch to a higher ISO setting. This enables you to choose a higher shutter speed.

TIP

Most monopods have a wrist strap. Use this in conjunction with your camera's neck strap to ensure that the camera doesn't go crashing to the ground while you're changing memory cards. After you photograph a scene with a monopod attached to your camera, collapse the extension tubes and tighten the locking collars before moving to another location. Alternatively, unloosen the mounting screw and take the camera off your monopod.

Figure 5-4: Capture photos of participants preparing for the event.

4. If the sport you are photographing has a support team, such as cheerleaders at a football game or a pit crew at an auto race, photograph them as they prepare for the event.

5. Photograph principals in the sport, such as the head coach conferring with the team and giving them final instructions before the heat of battle. If possible, zoom in to capture the range of emotions and the bond between the coach and athletes.

6. If you're photographing a team event, watch a practice session or warm-up. While watching the practice session, pay attention to the different athletes to get a feel for which athletes are more aggressive than others, which take risks, and which are rivals. This information enables you to track the athletes that will provide the most memorable shots.

7. Moments before the event starts, photograph individual athletes from a distance. Zoom in tight on the athlete's face to capture the mask of concentration as the athlete puts on his or her game face and mentally prepares for the event.

Capture Images of the Sporting Event

The type of event you're attending determines what vantage points and access you'll have to shoot photographs. If you're attending a stadium event, you'll be somewhat hampered by other spectators. However, if it is possible to leave your seat during the event, you can take pictures from different vantage points.

1. Photograph the start of the event. For example, if you're photographing a basketball game, zoom in and take a photograph of the tip-off. If you're photographing a football game, take a wide-angle shot of the opening kick-off, capturing the image a second or so after the ball leaves the kicker's foot.

2. Switch to continuous shooting mode, if your camera is so equipped. This enables you to take a sequence of images when the action gets hot and heavy; for example, when a soccer player rushes towards a one-on-one with the goalie.

3. Switch to sports or continuous focus mode, if your camera is so equipped.

4. Zoom in on the athletes, and follow the action.

5. Press the shutter button halfway while following the action through your viewfinder. Pan the camera to follow an athlete or group of athletes, and then press the shutter button when something interesting happens.

6. Photograph the event from different vantage points, if possible. This image shows a racecar slowing down for a hairpin turn. The photo was shot from a spectator mound with a telephoto zoom lens. The car was still going fast enough to capture the essence of motion. The image was shot with a slow shutter speed while panning the camera with the car.

7. Keep an eye on the sidelines for reactions from the coaches and teammates on the bench when someone scores.

TIP

When taking finish-line photos, switch to continuous shooting mode, if your camera is so equipped. Press the shutter button to capture a sequence of images as the athletes cross the finish line.

TIP

You can create memorable photos if you take pictures of athletes moments after the end of a competition. For example, a photograph of a marathon runner seconds after he crosses the finish line shows the toll a grueling physical competition takes on an athlete.

8. If you're photographing a timed event, take several pictures of the action as the clock winds down.

9. If you're photographing an event such as a triathlon, bicycle, or automobile race, take several pictures as the athletes cross the finish line, as shown in Figure 5-5.

Capture the Thrill of Victory and the Agony of Defeat

You can also capture some wonderful images after the event ends. Photograph the athletes at the awards ceremony. If a friend or relative receives a trophy, you can present them with a wonderful keepsake of their smiling face as they hold the trophy high in the air. At an automobile race, get close to the winner's circle, and capture images of the winning driver smiling and spraying the crowd with champagne. Take photographs of the losing team as well to capture the full range of emotions, from victory to defeat.

Figure 5-5: Capture a sequence of images of athletes crossing the finish line.

**TELLING THE STORY
OF THE EVENT**

When you get home from the event and download your pictures to your computer, you can get creative and assemble a journal of the event. Sort through your images, and arrange them in a logical order to show the athletes before, during, and after the event. Crop the Images as desired in your image-editing application, and delete any undesirable images. You can then arrange the images to create a slide show for computer viewing or for viewing from your Web site using the applications discussed in the latter part of this book.

TIP

When photographing a racecar slowing for a curve, practice panning a few cars before taking the photo. You'll have to slow down the pan in order to keep the car, which is rapidly decreasing speed, in the viewfinder.

TIP

Some digital cameras feature a sports mode that enables the camera to continually focus on a moving object. Refer to your camera manual to see if your digital camera is so equipped and, if while using this mode, your camera continually focuses on the subject.

Photograph an Automobile Race

If you're photographing an automobile race, the venue will determine how you photograph the event. If you're photographing a race on an oval track, you'll be photographing from the grandstands during the event and perhaps from the pits prior to the event. Use your camera's optical zoom to get as close to the action as possible. If the event promoters permit you to leave your seat and photograph through the fence, you can capture some close-ups of the cars as they zoom by. You can also take pictures of the pit crew. The following image uses the spokes of a wheel to frame a team member resting between pit stops.

If you're photographing a road race on a natural terrain course, roam from corner to corner. Many tracks have spectator mounds, which are wonderful vantage points for photography. When you photograph a road race, you can capture the essence of speed if you pan the camera, as outlined previously.

Shoot with a shutter speed of 1/125 of a second, and pan as the car races towards a hairpin curve to capture images like the one shown below.

QUICKSTEPS

USING BLUR CREATIVELY

If you're fortunate enough to photograph a world-class event, such as the Tour de France, where the cyclists often exceed 30 mph in sprints, you can capture wonderful photographs of the cyclists by panning, as outlined previously. However, if you're photographing athletes or cyclists that are not moving rapidly, you can blur both the athlete and the background to create an artistic impression of motion.

1. Switch to shutter priority mode.

2. Choose a slow shutter speed of 1/15 of a second or less.

3. Pre-focus the camera on a subject equidistant to the place where you'll take your picture, or switch to continuous focus mode, if your camera is so equipped.

4. Pan the camera with the athlete.

5. Press the shutter button to capture an artistic impression of motion, as shown here.

How to...

Chapter 6
Beyond Point-and-Shoot Photography

Creative people stretch the envelope. Whether you own a point-and-shoot digital camera, high-end digital camera, or digital SLR, you can take your photography to the next level by combining the techniques from previous chapters with the techniques you'll learn in this chapter. In this chapter, you'll learn advanced composition techniques, how to photograph during adverse conditions, and how to improvise to capture a picture in adverse conditions.

Creating Compelling Images using Advanced Composition

The difference between a humdrum photograph and an outstanding photograph is composition. Vacationers take pictures of stunning vistas like El Capitan in Yosemite National Park, yet their images pale in comparison to those

photographed by a master photographer such as Ansel Adams. By applying a few rules of composition, you can create pictures that will be the envy of your friends and neighbors.

Use Geometric Composition

One method you can use to create an interesting photograph is to create a geometric composition. When you size up a scene, look for geometric elements, such as rectangles, triangles, or circles. A geometric composition can also include curves that lead the viewer to a center of interest that is aligned according to the Rule of Thirds.

Use Rectangles and Squares as Compositional Elements

One of the keys to a successful photograph is examining a scene and using elements of the scene as part of your composition. If you have a scene with strong geometric elements, such as rectangles or squares, use them to your best advantage when composing the scene.

1. Walk around the scene and look for strong geometric elements. With a bit of work, you'll find geometric forms in key points of your scene.

2. Look for interesting objects to draw your viewer into the rectangular element that is your center of interest.

3. Take the picture. Figure 6-1 shows a geometric composition with a strong rectangular element. Notice the rectangular shape created by the sign and supports. The curve of the anchor draws the viewer into the scene, and the staff of the anchor is a strong vertical element that leads the viewer toward the sign. The rectangular shape frames the entry to the ship behind.

Compose a Scene with Circular Elements

Another geometric element you can use to compose your scenes is a circle. When you compose a scene with circular elements, you can look for repeating patterns or a series of circular elements. If you compose a scene with a series of

Figure 6-1: *Use geometric elements to compose your photos.*

TIP

If you're taking a head-and-shoulders portrait of someone wearing glasses with round lenses, have them hold a circular object, such as an antique pocket watch or magnifying glass. Tell your subject where to position his or her hand and the object to create a center of interest according to the Rule of Thirds. The viewer's eye will be drawn from the circular object to the subject's glasses.

circular elements, try to compose the scene so that one of the circular elements is positioned on a center of interest (Rule of Thirds). The viewer's eye will be drawn toward that element and be naturally drawn to the other circles in your picture.

1. Analyze the scene and look for the strongest circular element.

2. Compose the scene so that the strongest element intersects a point of interest (Rule of Thirds).

3. Take the picture. The following image is a scene that is strongly dominated by circular elements. The viewer's attention is first drawn to the girl in the white T-shirt. Then the viewer notices the round orange pumpkins

Compose a Picture Using Repeating Elements

If you use your digital camera frequently, you're always on the lookout for new and interesting things to photograph. You can create interesting pictures of repeating elements, such as sailboat masts or windmills.

1. Analyze the scene from all angles.

2. Compose the scene so that the repeating elements are aligned so that they draw your viewer into the picture.

3. Choose a vantage point that makes it readily apparent you want to draw your viewer's attention to the repeating elements.

4. Switch to aperture priority mode, and choose a small aperture (large f-stop number) for the greatest depth of field. If your camera is not equipped with aperture priority mode, switch to landscape or infinity mode.

5. Take the picture. This image shows a shot of sailboats in a marina. The composition is dominated by the vertical masts, which are juxtaposed by the red and green canvas sail covers.

Use Curves to Compose a Photograph

You can use curves to draw a viewer into your scene, as outlined previously. You can also pose a subject so that his or her body parts form gentle curves that attract the viewer's attention. A photograph showing a person with a gracefully arched back, curved limbs, and a tilted head is more interesting than one in which the person is ramrod-straight. Figure 6-2 shows the graceful curve of a young woman's neck. The photograph is also composed so that the red elements (lips, earring, and rose) form a triangle. In Figure 6-3, the curving shoreline draws the viewer into the picture.

*Figure 6-2: **Graceful curves can add interest to portraits.***

ADDING PERSPECTIVE TO A PHOTOGRAPH

When you're photographing a landscape or a cityscape on a clear day, you can see for miles. You can capture this sense of distance in a photograph when you add perspective. You add perspective when you compose the scene. For instance, if you're photographing a long city street, you can use the roofline to show perspective, which appears smaller in the distance. When you photograph a long city street, the cars parked on the side of the road appear to converge in the distance.

1. Zoom all the way out, or switch to a wide-angle lens if you're photographing with a digital SLR.

2. Switch to aperture priority mode, and choose a small aperture (large f-stop number) to ensure maximum depth of field. Switch to landscape or infinity mode if your camera doesn't have an aperture priority mode.

3. Compose the scene so that you've got either tall buildings in the foreground or a wide city street. If you're photographing buildings, the top of the building nearest the camera should fill the frame vertically or extend slightly beyond it to add a sense of grandeur to the picture. If you're shooting a city street, make sure the bottom of the frame shows the street from side to side for the same reason.

Continued . . .

TIP

If you're photographing an interesting scene, take a picture and then wait for something interesting to happen, such as a seagull flying into the scene. Then take another picture.

Figure 6-3: *Curves can be used to draw your viewer into the photograph.*

Compose a Photograph from Unique Vantage Points

Many beginning photographers shoot from eye level, which can result in perfectly wonderful photographs. However, when you shoot from above a subject, your photograph takes on a whole new meaning. The same is true if you photograph an object such as a vehicle or tall building from a crouching or kneeling position. The vehicle or building looks larger than life. Landscapes also benefit when you shoot from a crouching or kneeling position. The landscape looks more majestic, and if there are any mountains in the scene, they appear to be higher.

UICKSTEPS

ADDING PERSPECTIVE TO A PHOTOGRAPH *(Continued)*

4. If possible, get a tall person walking across the road as you shoot the picture. This will help enhance the feeling of perspective, especially if you shoot the photograph from a kneeling position.

5. Take the picture. This image shows a street scene in San Francisco's North Beach. The sloping roofline of the building on the right adds a sense of perspective and draws the viewer's eye to the man strolling down the sidewalk.

TIP

When photographing perspective, take the picture from a kneeling position or get closer to the ground to exaggerate the height of the buildings.

TIP

A viewer's attention is always drawn toward the brightest element in the scene.

TIP

When you photograph an individual from a bird's-eye view, make sure you're far enough away from the subject that you don't have to zoom out or use a wide-angle lens, which will distort the person's features.

Shoot a Photograph from Bird's-Eye View

If you're photographing a crowded street or a group of people, shoot from above the crowd. The resulting picture will be more interesting. Photographing a street scene from a rooftop or the window of a second-story hotel room will give you a whole new perspective. You'll be able to see more people from the elevated vantage point than if you photograph the scene from street level. You can also create interesting portraits of people from high vantage points. Landscapes are great candidates for photographing from a bird's-eye view as well. The following photograph was taken from a trail that rims the cliffs at Pt. Reyes National Seashore. When you see the beach in the distance and the cliff at land's end, it's obvious the photo was taken from a high vantage point.

TIP

Kneel to take the picture from a lower vantage point, so you are looking up toward the geometric form. Remember to keep the camera level; otherwise, you'll distort vertical lines, making them appear to lean inward. If you shoot with an ultra-wide angle lens (35-mm equivalent or less than 28 mm), you'll notice some barrel distortion, even when the camera is level.

QUICKSTEPS

TILTING THE CAMERA

Many photographers think there are only two orientations for a picture: landscape (horizontal) or portrait (vertical). But you can add a creative touch or a sense of whimsy to a photo if you tilt the camera diagonally. This technique is effective when you have strong diagonal elements in the scene.

1. Analyze the scene from different vantage points.

2. Look for any dominant diagonal elements, such as the gable end of a roof or a person's leg.

3. Tilt the camera so that the strong diagonal is parallel to one of the edges of the camera frame.

4. Alternatively, you can look for horizontal elements, such as the roadway in the image to the right. Tilt your camera so that the horizontal is diagonal from the top edge of the frame on one side to the bottom edge of the frame on the other side.

5. Press the shutter button fully to capture the image.

Shoot a Photograph from Snail's-Eye View

If you want something to look larger than life, photograph the subject from a crouching or kneeling position. When you do this, make sure you're far enough away from your subject so that you don't have to tilt the camera to fit the subject or scene in the frame. If you do, you'll distort the perspective of the scene and edges of buildings will appear to lean inward. The photographer was prone and very close to the car when he photographed the image on the right. The wide-angle lens made the headlight and front fender look huge, which was just the effect the photographer was after. The headlight is a point of interest that draws the viewer further into the picture.

Frame Your Subject

If you're photographing a person or an object, you can use architectural elements to create a frame around the person. When you create a frame around a subject, you leave no doubt in the viewer's mind what you are photographing.

1. Find a doorway, gate, or other architectural aspect with which to frame your subject. You can frame the subject's entire body with an architectural element, such as a doorframe or gate, or you can use foliage, such as palm fronds, to frame your subject. You can also frame a body part, such as a subject's head. In the image to the right, tree trunks and foliage frame a couple gazing out at a lake. The splash of light on the woman's hair and the man's red cap draws the viewer's eye into the scene.

2. Tell your subject the pose you'd like them to adopt. Just because you're framing them in a doorway doesn't mean they have to stand bolt upright. Have your subject move his or her arms and legs to adopt a graceful pose. If the doorway is open, the subject can turn sideways and lean against the doorway, resting one foot on the ground, and angle the other into the doorjamb while turning his or her face toward the camera. The subject's arms can be draped gracefully or artfully crossed underneath his or her chest. The image to the left is a picture of a young girl whose head is framed in a windowpane.

Create Soft Portraits and Still-Lifes

Your on-camera flash can help you capture images when there isn't enough available light to photograph with a fast shutter speed. However, on-camera flash is a harsh light. When you photograph a person with on-camera flash, the resulting photograph will show every wrinkle and imperfection on the

LOOKING FOR NATURAL VIGNETTES

Being observant is one of the key traits of a good photographer. If you've ever seen a photograph that has been transformed into a vignette, you know that the subject is the center of attention and there is an elliptical area around the subject that gradually fades to black. Sometimes, Mother Nature creates wonderful vignettes with light and shadows. With keen observation skills, a digital camera, and a bit of good luck, you can frame a subject in a natural vignette and create an image similar to the following.

person's face. Plus, when you work with on-camera flash, you'll have to deal with red-eye. A better lighting solution for portrait photography is available light. You'll have to use a tripod because of the slow shutter speed, but you'll get a better picture as a result.

Photograph by Window Light

You can create lovely portraits by using the available light from a window. The light is generally diffuse, unless it's early in the morning and the window faces the east. If there are curtains over the window, the light is filtered even further, resulting in a wonderfully soft, diffuse light that is perfect for taking portraits.

1. Mount your camera on a tripod.

2. Position your subject so that the light pouring through the window illuminates one side of his or her face.

3. Disable the camera flash.

4. Set the camera on auto-timer mode.

5. Move and adjust the tripod as needed to compose the scene. If desired, use the tripod controls to rotate the camera 90 degrees to achieve a vertical composition.

6. Press the shutter button halfway to establish focus. When you press the shutter button, you'll also be able to see the required exposure through your camera viewfinder or LCD monitor.

7. Remind your subject to sit perfectly still while the camera is recording the exposure. If you notice that the required exposure is going to be several seconds, tell your subject to remain still until you tell them the camera has finished taking the picture.

8. Press the shutter button fully. After you press the shutter button, the camera begins counting down. Do not touch the camera until the picture appears on your LCD monitor; otherwise, you'll shake the camera and get a blurry picture.

Fill In Shadows

The only problem you may encounter when shooting images with available light is that one side of your subject's face may be in deep shadow. This problem is exacerbated if you're relying solely on window light and the room in which you are photographing is dark. You could turn on a light, but then you're dealing with light sources that have different color temperatures, and your camera may have a hard time getting the white balance correct. The solution is to reflect some light into the shadowed areas of the scene. You can purchase a reflector from a local camera store, or you can build one yourself. If you purchase one from a camera store, you'll need a 42-inch round reflector if you're photographing the person from head to toe. If you're only photographing the person's head and shoulders, you can get by with a 22-inch reflector. Reflectors are white, silver, or gold. You can also create your own reflector by purchasing a large piece of white poster board or a piece of Styrofoam. Figure 6-4 shows an assistant aiming a 42-inch reflector at the subject to be photographed. The reflector has white fabric on one side and gold on the other. The reflector fabric unzips and is reversible. The reverse fabric colors are black (which is used to deepen shadows) and silver. The reflector collapses and fits in a 16-inch diameter bag.

Figure 6-4: **You use a reflector to bounce light onto your subject.**

Fill Shadows with a Reflector

1. If lighting conditions necessitate a slow shutter speed, set your camera on a tripod, and then position your subject as outlined previously.

2. Have a friend or family member hold the reflector and angle it so that the light is caught by the reflector and bounced back into the shadow side of your subject's face.

3. View the scene through the viewfinder, and tell your assistant which way to move the reflector. You'll be able to see the difference through the viewfinder.

4. Press the shutter button halfway to focus the scene.

5. Press the shutter button fully and release. The camera counts down and records the picture. This image was captured using available light under a tree. An assistant aimed a silver reflector at the model to bounce some light back into the heavy shadows on her face.

Photograph by Candlelight

Candlelight is another wonderful light source for available-light photography. The light from a candle is warm and golden, much like the light you'll find early in the morning or late in the afternoon.

1. Dim or extinguish any lights in the room, and then mount your camera on a tripod.
2. Switch to aperture priority mode, and choose the widest aperture (smallest f-stop number) available for your camera.
3. Seat your subject and place a lighted candle in front of him or her.
4. Switch to auto-timer mode.
5. Zoom in on your subject, and compose the picture.
6. Press the shutter button halfway to establish focus.
7. Press the shutter button fully and release. Your camera counts down and then takes the picture.

Deal with Adverse Conditions

Just because there's rain on the horizon or it's nighttime, don't pack your camera thinking you won't get a shot. If you're only a fair-weather daylight photographer, you're missing some wonderful opportunities for compelling pictures. When the

If you're forced to use on-camera flash when creating a portrait, you can diffuse the light by placing a piece of tissue over it. This results in a more flattering portrait, as the light is much softer.

COPING WITH ADVERSE LIGHTING

When you photograph in adverse conditions, you're generally dealing with adverse lighting conditions as well. This can be anything from dealing with lighting that is uneven, low lighting, or heavy shade. The following list shows some remedies for adverse lighting:

- Use fill-flash to fill in shadow when photographing in heavy shade or when the subject is backlit.
- Use a reflector to bounce light back into the shadow side of a subject's face.
- Increase the ISO setting to achieve a higher shutter speed.
- Use a tripod or monopod to steady the camera when photographing at slow shutter speeds in low-light situations.
- When you use a tripod to photograph a low-light scene, use the camera auto-timer to avoid camera movement when you press the shutter button. Alternatively, use a camera remote switch to trigger the shutter without touching the camera.
- Use your car headlights to add additional light when photographing in low-light situations.
- Use an off-camera flash with a swivel head, and angle the flash at the ceiling to bounce light on your subject and avoid harsh shadows. Make sure the ceiling is white; otherwise, the image will have a color cast.

weather's cloudy or overcast, the light is wonderfully diffuse. And when it rains, you get some lovely reflections of street lamps and buildings on the wet asphalt. If you're really lucky, after a rainstorm, you can get a picture-perfect rainbow with everything but the proverbial pot of gold. In the upcoming sections you'll learn some techniques for taking pictures in less-than-ideal conditions.

Photograph at Night

After the sun goes down and total darkness sets in, you have some wonderful picture-taking opportunities available. If you're vacationing in an exciting city, capturing images of the street lights and tourist attractions will provide memories for years to come. In order to photograph night scenes, you'll need to increase the camera ISO rating and/or use a tripod. When you increase the ISO setting, you may end up creating a bit of digital noise. However, sometimes a little digital noise can add to the excitement of a bustling night scene.

1. Mount your camera on a tripod. Alternatively, you can steady the camera using the methods described in "Shoot Low Shutter Speeds Without a Tripod."
2. If desired, choose a higher ISO setting to increase camera sensitivity.
3. Disable the camera flash.
4. Switch the camera to auto-timer mode.
5. Switch the camera to aperture priority mode, and choose a small aperture (high f-stop number) to achieve maximum depth of field. If your camera is not equipped with aperture priority mode, switch to landscape or infinity mode.
6. Mount your camera on a tripod.
7. Compose the scene and press the shutter button halfway to establish focus.
8. Press the shutter button fully and release. The camera begins counting down and takes the picture. The following image of Lakeland, Florida's Lake Morton was photographed at dusk using the steps in this procedure.

TIP

When taking a portrait of someone at night, you should use the camera flash only as described in Chapter 3. Most digital camera flash units are not powerful enough to capture night scenes.

TIP

If you're photographing a night scene, switch to landscape or infinity mode. If your camera has aperture priority mode, choose a small aperture (high f-stop number). The resulting exposure will be longer, but more of the scene will be in focus.

TIP

Instead of using auto-timer mode, you can purchase a remote switch, which enables you to trip the shutter button without touching the camera. Contact your local camera store to see if this accessory is available for your camera.

Photograph a Distant Thunderstorm

Electrical storms can be quite frightening when you're in one, but they can be quite beautiful when viewed from a distance and you can see lightning pop out of the billowing thunderheads. If you're patient and far enough away from the storm to be out of harm's way, you may be able to capture some fantastic images. Switch your camera to continuous shooting mode, and compose the scene. When you see the far-off lightning start to pop, hold the shutter button,

PHOTOGRAPHING IN INCLEMENT WEATHER

When the weather turns really foul, your best bet is to stay inside. Digital cameras are expensive and will quickly be ruined if subjected to moisture. Plus, it can be downright dangerous to photograph when a thunderstorm is nearby and the wind is howling. However, when the rain slackens to a drizzle or ends completely, you can capture some wonderful images. If you take photographs at night after a rainstorm, the glistening pavement will create great reflections of car lights, streetlights, neon signs, and so on. When you photograph night scenes during inclement weather, you'll have to steady the camera with a tripod or use a high ISO rating. The following image was photographed an hour or so after a rainstorm abated and the streets were almost dry. The camera was mounted on a tripod with the auto-timer enabled.

and your camera will take several pictures. With a bit of luck, you may get an image like the one shown here.

Improvise to Capture the Moment

Photography is rewarding, but it can also be a challenge, especially when you're far away from home or photographing in a public place such as a museum. When you're on vacation, you need to pack light, which means that goodies such as your tripod, off-camera flash, and other equipment that won't fit in your luggage are left languishing at home in the closet. When you're photographing in a museum, flash is often not allowed, as the intense light will damage the old paintings and other artwork.

PROTECTING YOUR CAMERA

When you photograph during inclement weather, it's imperative that you protect your camera from being exposed to moisture. If the weather turns really nasty, seek shelter. However, if you're photographing in a light mist or drizzle, first protect the photographer (that would be you) by donning raingear and then get some raingear for your camera. If your camera case is waterproof, store your camera there until you're ready to take a picture. Alternatively, you can tuck a small digital camera under your raincoat. You can protect your camera by draping a plastic bag over it, with a hole for the lens to poke through. Use a rubber band to seal the bag around the lens, as shown here. If the plastic bag is clear enough, you'll be able to compose the scene using the camera LCD monitor, which will be partially visible through the plastic. Another option is a waterproof housing for your camera.

TIP

You can purchase inexpensive beanbags, which can also be used to stabilize your camera when shooting at slow shutter speeds. An alternative is a zip-lock bag filled with uncooked rice or dried beans.

Other times, you may be in a situation that calls for a reflector, but yours is at home. What do you do? Improvise.

Shoot Low Shutter Speeds Without a Tripod

Sometimes, you're not permitted to use a flash, such as in a museum of fine art. There are other times when you want to photograph a scene, such as a busy plaza at night, but your on-camera flash is not powerful enough to capture the entire scene. The obvious answer is a tripod. But what do you do when you've left home without one? Find something to rest the camera on so it will remain steady during a long exposure.

1. Disable your camera flash. When you disable the flash, your digital camera increases the exposure time sufficiently to capture the scene.

2. Switch your camera to auto-timer mode.

3. Position your camera on a solid surface, such as a restaurant table or a park bench. If you want a vertical composition, press your camera against a solid object, such as the side of a building. Position the camera close to the edge of the solid surface, otherwise, you'll get part of the surface in your picture.

4. Compose the picture and then press the shutter button halfway to establish focus.

5. Press the shutter button fully, and wait for the camera to count down and take the picture. The resulting exposure may be quite long, so don't move the camera until you see the image appear in your LCD monitor. If you're holding the camera against the side of a building to achieve a vertical composition, hold the camera as tightly to the

wall as possible and remain as motionless as possible while the camera records the exposure. The image to the left is a horizontal composition of a night scene taken at Fisherman's Wharf in San Francisco. The camera was positioned on a stainless steel counter with the self-timer enabled. Notice the wonderful reflections in the countertop and the colorful glow from the neon signs.

Create a Makeshift Reflector

Reflectors are used to splash light back into the shadow side of a subject's face when you're photographing using available light without flash. Homemade reflectors made from sheets of Styrofoam are bulky and not practical when you're vacationing. With a little bit of ingenuity, you can create a makeshift reflector using objects you have on hand:

- Have a family member hold a bedsheet to bounce light back into your subject's face when creating a portrait using window light.

- Use your car's removable sun reflector as a reflector. Use the silver side when you need to bounce light into the scene and the gold side when you want to bounce warm light into the scene. When the image to the right was photographed, someone was angling the gold side of a sun reflector toward the subject to bounce warm light into the shadows.

- Have a friend or family member angle a white beach towel to catch the sunlight and reflect it toward a person you're photographing under a beach umbrella.

TIP

If the object on which you are resting your camera is not level, take the picture anyway. The resulting composition may be interesting, and it's better than no photo at all. After all, you can always level the image in your image-editing application after you download pictures to your computer.

TIP

An extra-large white T-shirt can be used when you need to reflect light back into a person's face.

Chapter 7
Editing Your Digital Images

Taking pictures is fun. Before digital cameras, you had to wait for the film to be processed before you saw the images. With digital cameras, you see the images you shoot almost immediately in the LCD monitor. After you take the pictures comes another fun part of the process: editing. The editing application I'll cover is Photoshop Elements 5.0, which, for all intents and purposes, functions as your digital darkroom. This chapter shows you how to get your images into your computer and then how to edit them to pixel perfection.

Get the Images Out of Your Camera

Before you can share your images or see full-sized versions of them, you must get them out of the camera and into your computer. The following sections show two methods for transferring images from camera to computer: the first uses the Universal Serial Bus (USB) cable supplied with most digital cameras; the second uses a card reader, which is a relatively inexpensive accessory you can purchase at any store that sells digital cameras.

Transfer Images to Your Computer

Your digital camera comes equipped with a USB port on the camera and a USB cable. When you connect the cable from your camera to an available USB port on your computer, you're ready to start transferring images. When you transfer images in this manner, you are using camera battery power. Thus, make sure the battery is fully charged before downloading the images. Transferring images from your digital cameras is slower than when using a card reader due to the fact that the camera's processor controls the transfer, whereas the computer controls the transfer when you use a card reader.

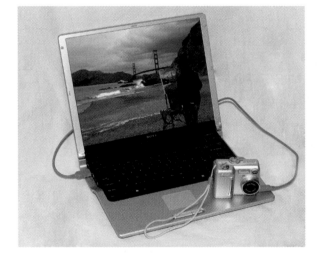

1. Start your computer and create a folder where you want to store the images.

2. Connect your camera to the USB cable supplied by your camera manufacturer.

3. Connect the USB cable to an available USB port on your computer, as shown here. What happens after you connect the camera depends on the operating system you use. Windows XP, for example, opens a dialog box with suggested actions. Choose the option that enables you to open a folder to display the image files on your memory card. If you're using a Macintosh, the default option will be to launch iPhoto and open the images in that application. Clear this option if you're using Photoshop Elements as your image-editing application. After doing this, your Macintosh operating system will recognize the camera as a removable hard drive.

4. Select all of the images.

5. Drag the images to the folder you created when you connected your camera to the computer. Or, if you're working on a Macintosh, drag the images from the removable hard drive to the folder you created in step 1.

6. Remove the camera from your system by disconnecting it from the USB cable.

Use a Card Reader

When you use a card reader to transfer images, the camera is not part of the operation. You remove the memory card from the camera and insert it directly into the card reader. The benefit of card readers is that you don't drain the camera battery. You can find a card reader that matches your type of memory card at most camera retailers for under $30.

1. Create a folder in your computer in which you'll store the images.

2. Remove the memory card from your camera.

3. Insert the memory card into your card reader. In Windows XP, a dialog box appears with suggested actions, as shown here. Choose the option to create a folder to view the image files on your memory card. On a Macintosh, the default action is to launch iPhoto and edit the images. If you're working with Photoshop Elements or another image-editing application, clear that option in iPhoto preferences—the Macintosh operating system will mount the card reader as a removable hard drive. If you have Photoshop Elements installed on a computer running Windows, the Adobe Photo Downloader launches. You can disable this by changing the camera or card reader preferences In the Photoshop Elements Organizer workspace.

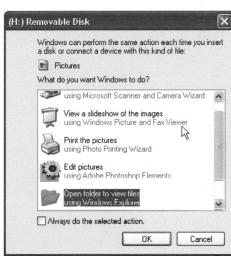

4. Select all of the images.

5. Drag the images from the folder (Windows) or removable hard drive (Macintosh) to the folder you created in step 1.

brightness, gamma (The way brightness is distributed across the intensity spectrum by a monitor, printer or scanner.), and white point (The temperature, measured in Kelvin, at which a monitor produces white light from equal parts of red, green, and blue light.) of the monitor. On a Windows-based computer, you can access the Adobe Gamma utility (shown here) through Control Panel. On a Macintosh, you can launch Adobe Gamma by choosing **Apple Menu | Control Panels | Adobe Gamma**. Note that you'll get your best results when using Adobe Gamma on a cathode ray tube (CRT) monitor, as Adobe Gamma was designed for CRT monitors and not LCD monitors.

TIP

For precise monitor calibration, consider purchasing a monitor calibration package. These contain a colorimeter, which attaches to your monitor, and a software application that monitors the results. When you calibrate your monitor, the colorimeter analyzes the images generated by the software as displayed on your monitor and sends the results back to the application. The application analyzes the results and then generates a profile for your monitor. Adobe Gamma relies on the user's subjective interpretation, whereas a good monitor calibration package gives consistent results, regardless of changes in lighting and other factors. As of this writing, you can find monitor calibration packages for as low as $69.95.

Introducing Photoshop Elements

Whenever you edit images, you generally perform many of the same tasks. To make these tasks easier, you should adopt a workflow. Some of the most common issues you'll be dealing with when editing digital images are sharpening, color correcting, and cropping images and then saving them. The following sections outline some of the tasks that typically need to be performed on digital images using Photoshop Elements Quick Fix and Full Edit modes.

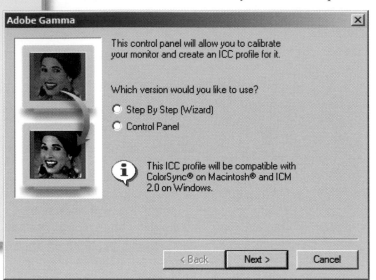

Launch Adobe Photoshop Elements 5.0

Photoshop Elements has a diverse selection of tools you can use to professionally edit an image. Many of the tools are intuitive, while others become easier to use as you gain familiarity with the application. The following sections will serve as an introduction to editing digital images in Photoshop Elements. To launch the application, choose **Start | Adobe Photoshop Elements 5** (Windows) or click the **Adobe Photoshop Elements** shortcut (Macintosh). After launching the application, the Welcome screen shown in the following image appears. From the Welcome screen, you can click a button to create a new file, browse for a file, connect to a camera or scanner, read common issues, or run a tutorial.

Photoshop Elements is a diverse program. The following chapters will cover the basics and show you some techniques for creating special effects. Unfortunately, I do not have enough room to cover every Photoshop Elements feature here. If the following chapters pique your curiosity and you'd like to learn more about Photoshop Elements, you'll find a variety of books on the application, either online or at your local bookstore. As of this writing, the current version of Photoshop Elements for Windows is version 5.0; for Macintosh, it's version 4.0.

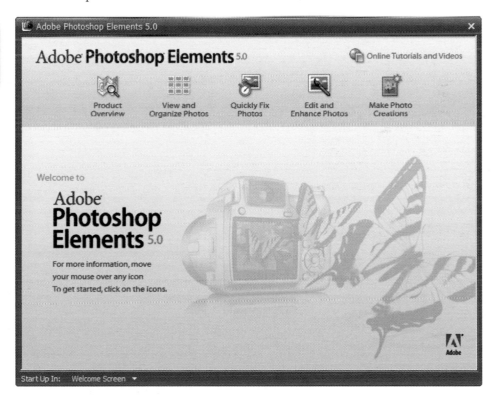

Edit Images in Quick Fix Mode

You can use Photoshop Elements to quickly fix a digital image. When you work in Quick Fix mode, Photoshop Elements calls the shots and applies a "smart fix" to the image. But if you don't like the results, you can modify the image by manually adjusting the lighting, color, and amount of sharpening applied. To edit an image in Quick Fix mode:

1. Launch Photoshop Elements.

2. Click the **Quickly Fix Photos** icon on the Welcome screen. After clicking the icon, the application loads the Quick Fix workspace, as shown in Figure 7-1.

Figure 7-1: ***You can improve most images using the Quick Fix mode in Photoshop Elements.***

3. Choose **File I Open**, navigate to the image you want to edit, and then open the file.

4. In the Smart Fix area, click **Auto**. Photoshop Elements applies what it deems are the optimal changes to fix your image.

5. Drag the **Amount** slider to apply a higher level of all fixes to the image.

6. Choose one of the following options from the View drop-down menu: **After Only, Before Only, Before And After (Portrait)**, or **Before And After (Landscape)**. The following image shows a photo being edited in Quick Fix mode with the Before And After (Landscape) view. The View menu is located in the lower-left corner of the workspace.

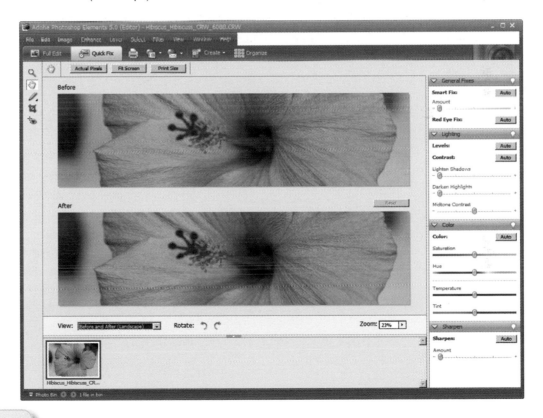

ADJUST LIGHTING

If the lighting changes applied with the smart fix are not acceptable, you can modify them to suit the needs of your photo. For example, you may need to lighten the shadow areas more or pump up the contrast. To adjust the lighting:

1. Click the **Reset** button. This changes the image to its original state.

2. If the image lacks detail in the shadow or highlight areas, click the **Auto** button next to Levels.

3. If the image has low contrast, click the **Auto** button next to Contrast.

4. To brighten the shadows more, drag the **Lighten Shadows** slider to the right.

5. To darken the highlights, drag the **Darken Highlights** slider to the right.

6. Drag the **Midtone Contrast** slider to the left to decrease contrast; drag to the right to increase contrast.

7. If the changes are acceptable, click the **Commit** button (it looks like a check mark). Alternatively, click the **Cancel** button to cancel all lighting changes.

ADJUST IMAGE COLORS

The smart fix attempts to correct any color cast the image may have. You can, however, manually modify the colors in an image.

1. Click the **Reset** button. This changes the image to its original state.

2. Click the **Auto** button next to Color. This automatically removes any color cast in the image.

3. Drag the **Saturation** slider to the right to increase image saturation; drag to the left to desaturate the image. If you drag the slider all the way to the left, the image becomes grayscale, similar to an image photographed with black-and-white film.

4. Drag the **Hue** slider to shift the colors in the image. Drag to the right to shift the colors to green; drag to the left to shift the colors to blue.

5. Drag the **Temperature** slider to the right to make the colors warmer (more red); drag to the left to cool the colors (more blue).

6. Drag the **Tint** slider to the right to tint the image green; drag to the left to tint the image magenta.

7. If the changes are acceptable, click the **Commit** button (it looks like a check mark). Alternatively, click the **Cancel** button to cancel all lighting changes.

TIP

If you want to convert an image to black and white, choose **Enhance | Convert To Black And White**. This command gives you options for different styles of photos, and you can modify the individual color channels (red, green, and blue), as well as image contrast, to get the desired effect.

Sharpen an Image

Images photographed with digital cameras may exhibit soft edges. As long as the subject in your image is in focus, you can sharpen an image in Quick Fix mode.

1. Choose the option from the View drop-down menu that matches the image you are sharpening. Choose Before And After Landscape if the image is wider than it is high, or choose Before And After Portrait if the image is higher than it is wide.

2. Click the **Actual Pixels** button. This increases the image magnification to 100 percent.

3. Click the **Auto** button next to Sharpen to apply the default amount of sharpening to the image.

4. Examine the edges of objects in the image. If you're satisfied with the sharpness of the image, click **Commit**. Alternatively, you can drag the **Amount** slider to increase the amount of sharpening.

Edit Images in Full Edit Mode

Some photographers prefer to have complete control when editing their images. If you fall into this group, you'll be happy to know that Photoshop Elements has a Full Edit mode, with a plethora of commands and tools for fine-tuning your images to pixel perfection. To edit images in Full Edit mode:

1. Launch Photoshop Elements.

2. Click the **Edit And Enhance Photos** icon on the Welcome screen. The application loads the Full Edit workspace, as shown in Figure 7-2. Alternatively, you can use the Quick Fix mode to apply your preliminary edits, and then click the **Full Edit** tab. As you can see, there is a wide variety of tools you can use to edit your images. When you see a triangle in the lower-right corner of a tool's icon, click it to reveal related tools. (A discussion of all the tools is beyond the scope of this book.)

Menu commands

Tools

Zoom tool

Hand tool

Marquee selection tools

Lasso tools

Magic Wand tool

Magic selection tools

Crop tool

Palette Bin

Photo Bin

*Figure 7-2: **In Full Edit mode, you have complete control over image editing.***

SHARPEN AN IMAGE IN FULL EDIT MODE

Some digital cameras don't produce a very sharp image. You can sharpen images in Photoshop Elements using several different commands. However, the best choice for sharpening an image is the Adjust Sharpness command, which

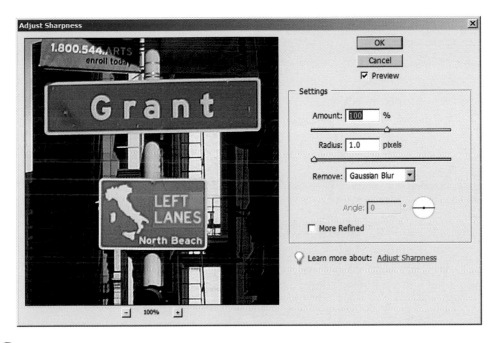

increases the contrast of edges in your image and makes the images look notably sharper.

1. Open the image you want to sharpen.

2. Choose **Enhance | Adjust Sharpness** to open the Adjust Sharpness dialog box, as shown here.

3. Drag the **Amount** slider to the right to determine the percentage of sharpening Photoshop Elements will apply to the image. Typically, a value between 100 and 150 percent works well for a large high-resolution image (8 inches by 10 inches and larger at 300 dpi) you plan on printing, and a value between 45 and 100 works well for a low-resolution image for monitor or Web site viewing. As you drag the slider, you can see what the sharpened image will look like in the Preview area, as well as in the actual image itself, if the Preview check box is selected. If you start to notice artifacts (bright halos and/or colored specks) around the edges in the image, you've over-sharpened. Drag the slider to the left until the artifacts disappear.

4. Drag the **Radius** slider to determine the distance in pixels from the edge where sharpening is applied. In most instances, the default value of 1 is perfect. If you increase the radius, pay attention to your image. If you increase the radius too much, you'll create artifacts in it, especially if there's any noise in the image.

5. Choose an option from the **Remove** drop-down menu. For photos of people, the Gaussian Blur option works well. If you're sharpening a photo of a landscape, choose the Lens Blur option.

6. Click **OK** to sharpen the image.

COLOR-CORRECT IMAGES

When you take a picture with your digital camera, the camera image sensor distributes the red, green, and blue pixels according to their brightness. An 8-bit image has 256 levels of red, green and blue. Dark pixels are at the low

CAUTION

If you apply high levels of sharpening to an image and then save it as a JPEG file with low quality, artifacts may appear.

TIP

If you're not happy with the results of any edit, choose **Edit | Undo** *<previously applied command>* before executing another command.

end of the scale, while the brightest pixels are at the high end of the scale. In certain conditions, a digital camera may not distribute the pixels properly, and your image may be lacking pixels at the low end of the scale. If this happens, the shadow areas of your image are not well defined. If your image is lacking pixels at the high end of the scale, highlight areas will not be well defined. You can correct for any deficiencies in levels by applying the Auto Levels command. However, when you correct levels, you may notice that the image acquires a color cast. For example, after applying the Auto Levels command, the image may look bluish or reddish. You can correct this deficiency with the Auto Color or Color Cast commands. The following image is in need of color correction:

APPLY THE AUTO LEVELS COMMAND

To correct an image that is lacking contrast or that appears washed out, choose **Enhance | Auto Levels**. After invoking the command, Photoshop Elements examines the distribution of pixels and then redistributes them as needed to correct for any deficiencies. The following image shows the image from

QUICKSTEPS

APPLYING THE AUTO COLOR COMMAND

To remove any color cast from an image, immediately after applying the Auto Levels command, choose **Enhance | Auto Color Correction**. The following illustration shows an image that has been color-corrected using the Auto Levels and Auto Color commands in succession.

If, after applying the Auto Levels and Auto Color commands, you notice the image does not have sufficient contrast, choose **Enhance | Apply Auto Contrast**.

QUICKSTEPS

REMOVING A COLOR CAST

The Auto Levels and Auto Color commands usually do a good job of balancing the color in an image, but sometimes, you may still notice a color cast; for example, the image may appear a bit bluish or reddish. You can use the Color Cast command to remove a color cast if you have areas in the image that you know are supposed to be pure black, nuetral gray, or pure white.

1. Choose **Enhance I Adjust Color I Color Cast** to open the Color Cast Correction dialog box, as shown below. Notice that the image being corrected has a red color cast.

2. Click the **Eyedropper** icon, and click a spot in the image that you know should be pure black, neutral gray, or pure white. In the case of this image, certain areas of the bird's plumage should be pure white.

3. Click **OK** to remove the color cast.

the "Removing a Color Cast" QuickSteps after the Auto Levels command was applied. It's always a good idea to use the Auto Levels and Auto Color commands in succession. After you apply the command, you may still not notice a visible difference.

ADJUST IMAGE COLOR

You can also manually adjust the color of an image. Photoshop Elements has several commands for adjusting color. A complete tutorial on every command is beyond the scope of this book, but in this section, I'll cover the Color Variations command, which makes it possible for you to adjust color with several visual references.

1. Open the image that needs color adjustment.

If the color cast isn't corrected by clicking the spot you thought would solve the problem, hold down the **CTRL** key (Windows) or hold down the **COMMAND** key (Macintosh), and click another area in the image. Click as often as needed until the image looks good to you.

If your image needs a lot of color adjustment, use the default amount setting. As the image gets closer to the desired result, drag the **Amount** slider to the left to apply more subtle adjustments to the image.

2. Choose **Enhance | Adjust Color | Color Variations** to open the Color Variations dialog box. The following illustration shows a picture with a couple of variation adjustments applied. On the left is the "before" image; on the right is a preview with adjustments applied.

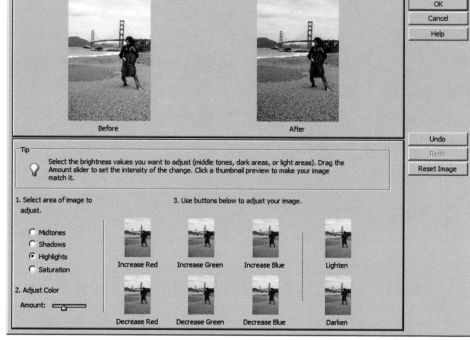

3. Select the tonal range you want to adjust. Your options are Midtones, Shadows, and Highlights.

4. Drag the **Amount** slider to determine how much color adjustment is applied. If you only need subtle color adjustments, drag the slider toward the left. If you need to apply larger amounts of color adjustment, drag the slider toward the right.

5. Click one of the thumbnails to have the adjusted image match the variation. After you apply a variation, the thumbnails are adjusted accordingly. If desired, you can apply additional color variations to further change the image. The After image preview updates each time you click a thumbnail.

TIP

Click the **Undo** button to undo the last variation you applied; you can click it multiple times to undo multiple variations. Click the **Redo** button to redo the last variation; you can click it as needed to redo multiple variations. Click the **Reset** button to restore the image to the same state as when the Color Variations dialog box was opened.

TIP

You can adjust more than one tonal range if needed. After adjusting one tonal range, select the option for the next tonal range you need to adjust.

6. Click the **Lighten** or **Darken** variation to lighten or darken the tonal range you are adjusting.

7. Click the **Saturation** option if the saturation of the colors in your image needs to be adjusted, and then click the **Less Saturation** or **More Saturation** variation, as shown below.

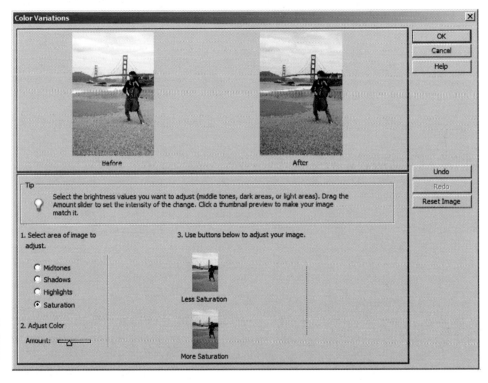

8. After the image is adjusted as desired, click **OK** to apply the changes.

ADJUST BRIGHTNESS AND CONTRAST

If desired, you can manually adjust brightness and contrast in an image. You adjust these parameters when an image is noticeably too bright or too dark, or lacks contrast, or if you want to create a special effect with an image.

1. Open the image you want to adjust.

TIP

To add some sparkle to a slightly washed-out image, choose the **Brightness/Contrast** command. Drag the **Contrast** slider a small increment to the right, and then drag the **Brightness** slider a small increment to the left. Tweak each slider until the image has the contrast and sparkle you seek.

2. Choose **Enhance | Adjust Lighting | Brightness/Contrast** to display the Brightness/ Contrast dialog box, shown in the above illustration.

3. Drag the **Brightness** slider to the right to make the image brighter; drag to the left to darken it. As you drag the slider, you'll see the changes in your image, provided the Preview check box is selected.

4. Drag the **Contrast** slider to the right to increase contrast; drag to the left to decrease contrast.

5. Click **OK** to apply the change.

Adjust Lighting

When your digital camera's firmware (a set of instructions programmed into camera memory that determines how the camera processes images) does everything right, it's a wonderful thing. It's also a wonderful thing when the photographer knows the camera like the back of his or her hand and knows just what to do when encountering a situation where the camera may not be able to compensate for a difficult situation, like a bright sky in the background or heavy shadow. If either scenario fails, the photographer (that would be you) still has options to change lighting by using the Photoshop Elements Shadows/Highlight command.

ADJUST SHADOWS AND HIGHLIGHTS

You use the Shadows/Highlight command when editing an image where the shadows or highlights need to be adjusted. For example, if the subject in your image is in shadow, you can reveal detail by brightening the shadows. If the camera exposed the image for the main object in your scene and the highlights are too bright, you may be able to reveal detail by darkening the highlights. The beauty of this command is that the midtones are not affected.

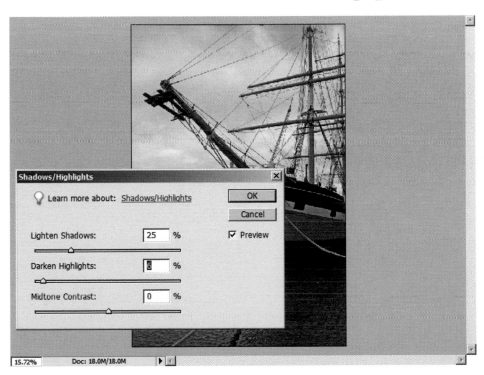

1. Open the image you want to adjust.

2. Choose **Enhance | Adjust Lighting | Shadows/Highlights** to open the Shadows/Highlights dialog box, as shown.

3. Drag the **Lighten Shadows** slider to the right to reveal more detail in the shadow areas of your picture. Note that the default settings will cause a loss of contrast or a milky look in the image. If this occurs, drag the slider to the left until you achieve an acceptable compromise.

4. Drag the **Darken Highlights** slider to the right to reveal more detail in the highlight areas of your picture. Note that you cannot recover details when highlights are totally blown out to white.

5. Drag the **Midtone Contrast Slider** to the right to increase contrast or to the left to decrease contrast.

6. **Click OK** to apply the changes.

TIP

To find help on a given task, type a question in the text field next to the Help menu.

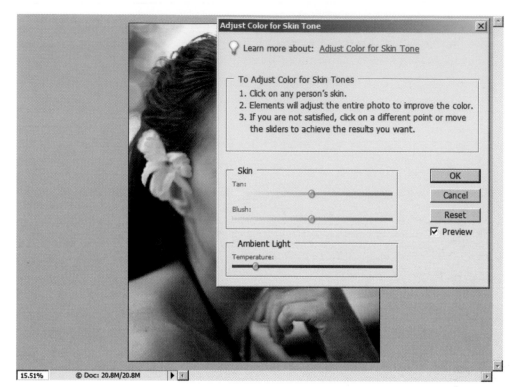

ADJUST SKIN TONES

If you photograph portraits, you may notice that the skin tones don't look right in certain lighting conditions. You can easily fix a photo by adjusting the image color for the subject's skin tone.

1. Open the image you want to adjust.

2. Choose **Enhance | Adjust Color | Adjust Color For Skin Tone** to open the Adjust Color For Skin Tone dialog box.

3. Click an area of the subject's skin. Photoshop Elements adjusts the colors based on the area you clicked. If you don't like the results, click another area. Alternatively, you can drag the **Tan** and **Blush** sliders to modify the subject's skin tone. If you're satisfied with the results, go to step 5.

4. Drag the **Temperature** slider to change the color of the ambient light. Drag to the left to cool the image; drag to the right to warm the image.

5. Click **OK** to apply the changes.

Process RAW Images

Many high-end digital cameras and all digital SLRs can capture images in the RAW format. You do this by choosing the option on your camera menu. Your camera does not process images captured in the RAW format. Instead, you get the image that the camera image sensor recorded, which gives you more data with which to work. If your camera can capture images in the RAW format, a utility to process the images and save them as TIFF or JPEG files was included with your camera. To process the RAW images, install the software and follow the instructions to process your RAW images. Photoshop Elements 5.0 offers support for the RAW format. The application ships with the Camera Raw plug-in, which is constantly updated when new cameras come on the market. To process RAW images with Photoshop Elements:

1. In either Quick Fix or Full Edit mode, open the RAW file you want to process. This opens the Camera Raw dialog box. By default, Photoshop Elements automatically

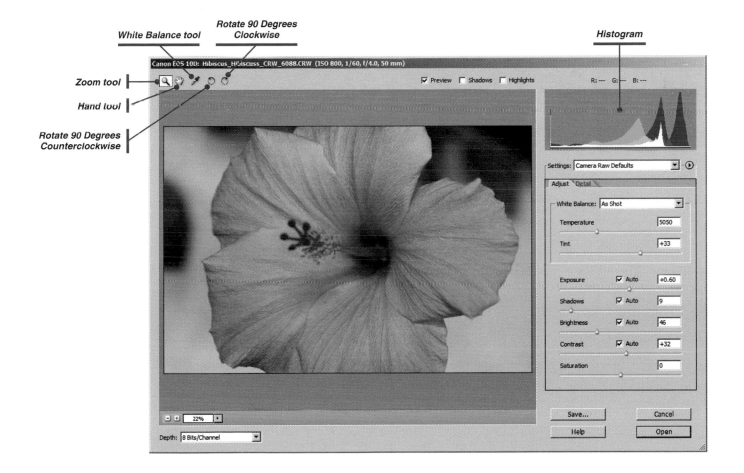

TIP

Select the **Temperature** value, and press the **UP ARROW** key to increase the value by 50 degrees Kelvin, or press the **DOWN ARROW** key to decrease the value by 50 degrees Kelvin. Press **SHIFT+UP ARROW**, to increase the value by 500 degrees Kelvin, or press **SHIFT+DOWN ARROW** to decrease the value by 500 degrees Kelvin.

TIP

Select the **Tint** value, and press the **UP ARROW** key to increase its value by 1, or press **SHIFT+UP ARROW** to increase its value by 10. Press the **DOWN ARROW** key to decrease its value by 1, or press **SHIFT+DOWN ARROW** to decrease its value by 10.

TIP

If you don't have large areas of your image where details are blown out in all color channels, you can recover details in an overexposed image by dragging the Exposure slider to the left. Press the **ALT** key (Windows) or the **OPTION** key (Macintosh) while dragging the slider. The overexposed areas will be designated by a red, green, or blue overlay. You may also see other colors, which indicates that two color channels are blown out. Drag the **Exposure** slider until the colors begin to disappear. Don't reduce the exposure by more than 0.75; the end results won't look natural.

applies the settings it deems best for the image. If the default settings are acceptable, click **Open** to work with the processed image in Photoshop Elements. To tweak the settings, continue with the steps in this procedure.

2. To adjust the white balance, select the **White Balance** tool, and click an area that should be pure white, neutral gray, or pure black. Alternatively, drag the **Temperature** slider to the right to increase the color temperature of the light or to the left to decrease the color temperature of the light. The color temperature value is measured in degrees Kelvin. Drag the **Tint** slider to fine-tune the color balance. Drag the slider to the left to add a green tint to the image; drag to the right to add a magenta tint.

3. Drag the **Exposure** slider to the right to increase exposure; drag to the left to decrease exposure. As you drag the slider, hold down the **ALT** key (Windows) or the **OPTION** key (Macintosh) to display a black overlay on the image. If you see a color appear when you drag the slider, you are blowing out highlights in that color channel. If you see solid white, you are blowing out all details to white. As you drag the Exposure slider, the histogram changes.

4. Drag the **Shadows** slider to the right to darken shadow areas; drag to the left to lighten them. As you drag the slider, hold down the **ALT** key (Windows) or the **OPTION** key (Macintosh) to display a white overlay on the image. If you see a color appear when you drag the slider, you are losing shadow detail in that color channel. If you see solid black, you are losing all shadow detail in that area of your photo.

5. Drag the **Brightness** slider to the right to brighten the image; drag to the left to darken it. In essence, this setting changes the midtone values of the image. You can, however, brighten an image too much, and it will appear as though all detail in the highlight areas of your image are lost.

6. Drag the **Contrast** slider to the right to increase contrast; drag to the left to decrease contrast. This setting increases contrast by increasing the brightness of highlights and darkening shadow areas of the image, while leaving the middle of the tone curve unchanged. If you picture an S-curve, you'll get an idea of how the Contrast control works. Note that the middle of the tone curve is determined by the Brightness value.

7. Drag the **Saturation** slider to the right to increase color saturation; drag to the left to decrease color saturation.

TIP

To increase the Shadows, Brightness, Contrast, or Saturation value by 1, press the **UP ARROW** key. To decrease the Shadows, Brightness, Contrast, or Saturation value by 1, press the **DOWN ARROW** key. To increase the Shadows, Brightness, Contrast, or Saturation value by 10, press **SHIFT+UP ARROW** key. To decrease the Shadows, Brightness, Contrast, or Saturation value by 10, press **SHIFT+DOWN ARROW KEY**.

TIP

Don't delete your RAW files after processing them. RAW image files are like film negatives. You can reprocess them using different settings as needed to create new images. Archive your RAW image files to a CD or DVD for future use.

TIP

To increase magnification of the image, choose an option from the Magnification Window drop-down menu, which is in the lower-right corner of the Camera Raw dialog box. Alternatively, you can press **CTRL+PLUS** sign (+) in Windows or **CMD+PLUS SIGN** (+) in Macintosh to increase magnification.

8. Click the **Detail** tab. The Camera Raw dialog box reconfigures, as shown below.

9. Drag the **Sharpness** slider to the right to increase the amount of sharpening applied to the image; drag to the left to decrease it. Some photographers prefer to apply sharpening in Photoshop Elements, as it provides more control over the process.

10. Drag the **Luminance Smoothing** slider if your image appears grainy due to digital noise, which usually occurs when an image is shot at a high ISO setting. If you use a high Luminance Smoothing value, you lose image detail. When you apply luminous smoothing, view the image at 100 percent, and then use the **Hand** tool to pan to an area of the image that contains shadows. This is where noise will be most noticeable.

11. Drag the **Color Reduction** slider if your image shows signs of color noise. Color noise looks like random speckles of color, and is most noticeable in shadow areas of the image.

12. Click **Open** to open the image in Photoshop Elements. You can then edit the image using Photoshop Elements commands and save the file in a format supported by the application. Your original RAW file is unaltered. All changes you make in the Camera Raw dialog box are saved in a separate file known as a sidecar file.

DECIPHERING HISTOGRAMS

A histogram is a visual reference of the distribution of pixels in the tonal ranges of an image. You can use a histogram to monitor the results of your edits in Photoshop Elements and in the Camera Raw dialog box. The left side of the histogram displays the shadows, the middle displays the midtones, and the right side of the histogram displays the highlights. The following image shows an image histogram. The spike on the left side of the histogram indicates that some detail in the shadow area has been lost. If you see a histogram with a spike on the right side, it means that some highlight details have been blown out. A histogram is displayed in the upper-right corner of the Camera Raw dialog box. To display a histogram in Photoshop Elements, choose **Window** | **Histogram**.

Histogram	More ▶

Channel: RGB

Source: Entire Image

Mean:	174.98	Level:	246
Std Dev:	53.89	Count:	85387
Median:	189	Percentile:	99.31
Pixels:	6291456	Cache Level:	1

Hold down the **SHIFT** key to constrain a rectangular marquee selection to a square or to constrain an elliptical marquee selection to a circle. Remember to release the mouse button prior to releasing the **SHIFT** key, or the selection will no longer be constrained.

Create Selections

In the previous sections, you learned how to make adjustments to your digital images. However, sometimes you only need to adjust part of an image, for example, applying the Brightness/Contrast command to just the person in the image and not the background. You can apply an adjustment, or for that matter a filter (which will be covered in Chapter 8), to a portion of an image after you make a selection. You have several tools available for selecting portions of an image, which will be discussed in the upcoming sections.

Create a Rectangular or Elliptical Selection

1. Open the image you want to edit.

2. Select the **Rectangular Marquee** tool to create a rectangular selection, or select the **Elliptical Marquee** tool to create a circular selection.

3. Click inside the image, and drag to size the marquee. As you drag, you'll see moving lines around the border of your selection as currently sized. The moving border is often referred to as an "army of marching ants."

4. Release the mouse button when the selection is the desired size.

Create Selections with the Lasso Tools

You can create a freeform selection with the Lasso tools. There are three Lasso tools: the Lasso tool, the Polygonal Lasso tool, and the Magnetic Lasso tool. The Lasso tools reside as a single icon on the toolbox. To reveal them, click the triangle in the lower-right corner of the last used Lasso tool to reveal a fly-out menu. Click the desired tool to make it the active Lasso tool:

- The **Lasso** tool enables you to draw a freeform selection by clicking and dragging. If you're good with a mouse, you can create precise selections in this manner.

- The **Polygonal Lasso** tool enables you to define the shape of a selection by clicking to add points. Photoshop Elements creates a line between the two points. When you're finished defining the shape of the selection, you click the first point to close it.

- The **Magnetic Lasso** tool enables you to create a complex path. The tool creates points as you move your cursor over the edge of a shape.

CREATE FREEFORM SELECTIONS WITH THE LASSO TOOL

When you create a selection with the Lasso tool, you use the mouse to draw a freeform selection around the area you want to select.

1. Select the **Lasso** tool.

2. In the options bar, which appears below the Full Edit and Quick Fix tabs, type a value between 0 and 250 in the Feather field. This setting determines how much feathering Photoshop Elements applies to the selection. When you feather a selection, you determine how soft the edge of the selection will be. The default value of 0 produces a hard-edged selection, while higher values gradually blend the selection into the surrounding pixels.

3. Accept the default Anti-Alias option. Anti-aliasing smoothes the edge of the selection.

4. Click to define the starting point of your selection and, while holding the mouse button, drag around the area you want to select.

5. Release the mouse button to close the selection. An army of marching ants defines the border of your selection, as shown here.

CREATE SELECTIONS WITH THE POLYGONAL LASSO TOOL

When you create a selection with the Polygonal Lasso tool, you click to define each point of the selection. Photoshop Elements then connects the points to define the boundary of the selection.

1. Select the **Polygonal Lasso** tool.

2. In the options bar, type a value between 0 and 250 in the Feather field. This setting determines how much feathering Photoshop Elements applies to the selection. When you feather a selection, you determine how soft the edge of the selection will be. The default value of 0 produces a hard-edged selection, while higher values gradually blend the selection into the surrounding pixels.

3. Accept the default Anti-Aliasing option. Anti-aliasing smoothes the edge of the selection.

4. Click to define the first point of the selection.

5. Click to define each additional point of the selection.

6. Click the first point to close the selection. The following image shows a fairly precise selection of the model's cowgirl hat made with the Polygonal Lasso tool.

CREATE SELECTIONS WITH THE MAGNETIC LASSO TOOL

You can make precise selections with the Magnetic Lasso tool. As the name implies, the tool develops a magnetic attraction for the edge of the object you want to select. What actually happens is the tool detects the difference in pixel color as you drag it over an edge, creating points as needed to define the selection. You specify the sensitivity of the tool and the distance from your cursor used to detect the edge.

1. Select the **Magnetic Lasso** tool.

2. In the options bar which can be found below the Photoshop Elements toolbar, set the following parameters:

   - Type a value between 0 and 250 in the Feather field. This setting determines how much feathering Photoshop Elements applies to the selection. When you feather a selection, you determine how soft the edge of the selection will be. The default value of 0 produces a hard-edged selection, while higher values gradually blend the selection into the surrounding pixels.

   - Accept the default Anti-Aliasing option. Anti-aliasing smoothes the edge of the selection.

   - Type a value between 1 and 40 in the Width field. This setting determines how far from your current cursor position Photoshop Elements will search for different color pixels.

   - Type a value between 1 and 100 in the Edge Contrast field. High values detect edges that contrast sharply from surrounding pixels, while low values detect edges with lower contrast edges.

   - Type a value between 0 and 100 in the Frequency field. This determines how quickly Photoshop Elements adds points as you move your cursor over an edge. Specify a high value to anchor points more quickly.

3. Move your cursor over the object you want to select, and then click to define the starting point.

4. Drag your cursor over the edge. As you trace the edge with your cursor, Photoshop Elements adds points that snap to the edges based on the settings you specify in the options bar. The selection can be modified using one of the menu commands or tools. The selection can also be copied to the Clipboard and composited into another image.

5. To close the selection, do one of the following:

   - Drag your cursor over the first point, and release the mouse button.

   - Move your cursor toward the starting point, and then double-click to close the selection.

   - To close the selection with a straight point between your current cursor position and the first point of the selection, hold down the **ALT** key (Windows) or **OPTION** key (Macintosh), and then double-click. Closing a selection in this manner is useful when you're selecting an object that ends at the border of the image, such as the torso of a person in a head-and-shoulders portrait.

TIP

If the object you are selecting has well-defined edges, specify high Width and Edge Contrast settings. This will enable you to make a precise selection while roughly tracing the border of the object you're selecting. If the object you are selecting does not have well-defined edges, specify low Width and Edge Contrast settings, and carefully trace the border of the object.

TIP

To temporarily activate the Lasso tool while making the selection, press down the **ALT** key (Windows) or the **OPTION** key (Macintosh), and drag. Release the **ALT** key (Windows) or **OPTION** key (Macintosh) to revert back to the Magnetic Lasso tool.

TIP

To manually create a point while using the Magnetic Lasso tool, press the **ALT** key (Windows) or **OPTION** key (Macintosh).

Create Selections with Other Tools

Creating selections confounds many Photoshop Elements beginners. It can be frustrating to create a precise selection. However, with a bit of patience and practice, you can create selections of parts of the image you need to manipulate or to cut a person out of one photo and insert him or her in another. That's why you have such a diverse choice of selection tools in Photoshop Elements. The next sections will cover the remaining selection tools.

Create Selections with the Magic Wand Tool

You use the Magic Wand tool to create a selection based on pixel color. This tool is handy if you photograph someone against a solid-color wall and you want to cut the person from the background for use in another photo. You can specify how close in color the pixels must be before the tool adds them to a selection.

1. Select the **Magic Wand** tool.

2. In the options bar, type a value between 0 and 255 in the Tolerance field. A low value selects pixels that are closer in color, while a high value selects pixels from a wider range of colors.

3. Accept the default Anti-Alias and Contiguous options. Anti-aliasing smoothes the edge of the selection, and Contiguous confines the selection to adjacent pixels.

4. Click the **All Layers** check box to create a selection using all layers.

5. Click the color you want to select. Photoshop Elements creates an army of marching ants that defines the boundary of the selection, as shown here.

TIP

After making a selection, hold the Shift key and use any selection tool to add to the image. If you're using the Magic Wand tool to add to a selection, you can modify the Tolerance setting as needed, when selecting a different color or area.

TIP

If the selection isn't as desired, enter a different value in the Tolerance field, and try again. Enter a smaller value if the tool selected too many pixels; enter a higher value if the tool didn't select enough pixels.

Create Selections with the Selection Brush Tool

You can create a selection using the Selection Brush tool. You use this tool to paint over the pixels you want to select. You can also use this tool to create a mask to protect part of an image. When you use the Selection Brush tool, you specify the thickness of the brush as well as the brush tip.

1. Select the **Brush Selection** tool.

2. In the options bar, choose a brush shape from the drop-down menu.

3. Select one of the following mode options:
   - **Selection** paints over the pixels you want to select.
   - **Mask** paints a mask over pixels you want to protect.

4. Drag over the pixels you want to select or mask.

5. Release the mouse button when the desired pixels are selected. This illustration shows a mask made with the Selection Brush tool. For the purpose of this illustration, the selection was made in Mask mode so it would be easier to see. If the selection had been made in Selection mode, an army of marching ants would surround the selection.

Create Selections with the Magic Selection Brush Tool

Yet another way to make a selection is with the Magic Selection Brush tool. This tool is simplicity at its best. The tool recognizes like colors in an area in which you draw or scribble with the tool.

1. Select the **Magic Selection Brush** tool.

2. In the options bar, choose a color for the brush tip. The default color (red) works well in most instances.

3. In the options bar, specify the width of the brush tip.

4. Scribble inside the area you want to select. When you release the mouse button, Photoshop Elements creates a selection based on the colors in the area in which you used the tool. After the selection is created, the tool icon has a plus sign, which indicates you can add to the selection by using the tool in another area. You can also remove areas from the selection by clicking the Magic Selection Brush icon with a minus sign and then scribbling inside the area that you want to remove from the selection. The following image shows a selection made using the Magic Selection Brush tool. The selection is defined by a moving dashed line, which some photographers refer to as an army of marching ants.

Edit Selections

Creating a precise selection is like sculpting. The sculptor chips away stone to find the artwork within, just as you select a portion of your image to create a great photo. However, unlike sculpting, when you create a selection and select too much or too little, you can easily add to or subtract from it. To edit a selection, do one of the following:

- To add to a selection, select the desired tool. Hold down the **SHIFT** key, click inside the selection, drag outside of the selection to define the area you want to add to it, and release the mouse button. You can add multiple areas to the selection as long as you hold down the **SHIFT** key.

- To remove pixels from a selection, select the desired tool. Hold down the **ALT** key (Windows) or **OPTION** key (Macintosh), click outside the selection, and drag inside the selection to define the pixels you want removed. Release the mouse button to complete editing the selection. You can trim multiple areas from a selection as long as you hold down the **ALT** or **OPTION** key.

- To remove a selection that is no longer needed, choose **Select | Delete Selection**. Or you can use the keyboard shortcut **CTRL+D** (Windows) or **COMMAND+D** (Macintosh).

- To select the inverse of a selection, choose **Select | Inverse**. For example, if you've created a selection of a person, selecting the inverse will select everything but the person.

- To feather a selection, choose **Select | Feather**. After choosing this command, a dialog box appears, asking you for the number of pixels by which you want to feather the selection. When you feather a selection, the pixels in the selection are gradually blended into the pixels surrounding it by the specified distance.

- To save a selection for future use, choose **Select | Save Selection**. After choosing this command, a dialog box appears, prompting you for a name for the selection. Enter the name for the selection, and click **OK**.

- To load a saved selection, choose **Select | Load Selection**. After choosing this command, a dialog box appears, prompting you to select the mask to load.

Crop Images

Sometimes, you get it just right and take the perfect picture. Other times, you get more than you need. You can easily remove unwanted parts of an image using the Crop tool.

1. Select the image that you want to crop.

2. Select the **Crop** tool.

3. Drag inside the image to define the area that you want to crop from it.

4. Release the mouse button. Photoshop Elements draws a bounding box around the selected area. The area outside the bounding box (the part that will be cropped out) is 75 percent opacity black in color, as shown in the following illustration.

5. To modify the crop marquee, do one of the following:

   - Drag a handle at any corner to resize the width and height of the crop marquee. Hold down the **SHIFT** key while dragging to resize the crop marquee proportionately.

   - Drag a handle in the middle of the right or left side to resize the width of the crop marquee.

   - Drag a handle at the top or bottom to resize the height of the crop marquee.

   - Click inside the crop marquee, and drag to change its position.

6. Press **ENTER** or **RETURN** to crop the image. Alternatively, you can click the **Commit** button (it looks like a check mark) on the border of the crop marquee.

Resize Images

When you resize an image, you are resampling it. In other words, Photoshop Elements is taking all of the image data and redrawing the pixels so that the image is the desired size. When you choose a smaller size, Photoshop Elements does an admirable job of resizing the image. However, when you ask the application to increase the size of the image, Photoshop Elements increases the

TIP

If you're sending the image via e-mail or preparing it for a Web site, type <u>72</u> in the resolution field, as this is the resolution of a computer monitor.

TIP

If you increase the resolution of an image, clear the **Resample Image** check box. If you try to increase the resolution of an image with this check box selected, Photoshop Elements will increase the pixel dimensions of the image without changing the document size in inches, and degradation will result. When you clear this check box, Photoshop Elements does not change the document size in pixels, but decreases the image size in inches to reflect the higher resolution.

size of each pixel, which inevitably leads to degradation of the image. Therefore, upsizing an image is not recommended. When you resize an image, you can also change the image resolution.

1. Choose **Image** I **Resize** I **Image Size** to open the Image Size dialog box.

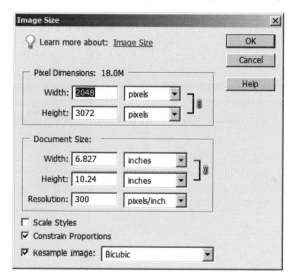

2. Click the **Constrain Proportions** check box. This resizes the image proportionately, which means you need to enter only the width or height, and Photoshop Elements will calculate the size of the other dimension to resize the image proportionately.

3. Type a value in the Resolution field, or accept the current image resolution.

4. Type the desired width or height into the applicable field. If you type a dimension in the Pixel Dimensions section, Photoshop Elements will supply the proper dimensions for the Document Size section, and vice versa.

5. Click **OK** to resize the image.

Save Edited Images

After you've done all your editing and your image is pixel perfect, you can save the image for future use. Photoshop Elements has two commands for saving a file: Save and Save As. Use the Save command to save a file in its original format, and use the Save As command when you want to save the file in a different format.

USE THE SAVE COMMAND

1. Choose **File | Save** to save the image in its native format and in the same folder from which it was opened.

2. Choose **File | Close** to close the image.

USE THE SAVE AS COMMAND

1. Choose **File | Save As** to open the Save As dialog box.

QUICK**FACTS**

UNDERSTANDING FILE FORMATS

A complete dissertation of each file format supported by Photoshop Elements is beyond the scope of this book. The following list shows some of the commonly used formats for images that will be printed or distributed on the Web:

- **Photoshop (*.psd, *.pdd)** Save an image in this format when you want to preserve masks, layers, and selections for future editing.

- **BMP (*.bmp, *.rle, *.dib)** Save an image in this format if you're going to use it in an application that supports it. Layers cannot be saved when you use the BMP format. This format is suitable for printing high-resolution images.

- **JPEG (*.jpg, *.jpeg, *.jpe)** Save an image in this format if you're going to display it on a Web site or share it with someone via e-mail. When you save an image in this format, you can specify an image quality from 0 (low-quality image, small file size) to 12 (high-quality image, large file size). When you specify a quality setting lower than 12, the image is compressed, which means that certain color information will be lost in order to achieve a smaller file size. High-resolution JPEG files are a good choice if you're going to have your images printed by a drugstore or kiosk that prints digital images.

Continued . . .

2. Click the **Save In** down arrow, and navigate to the folder in which you want to store the image.

3. If desired, enter a new name for the file.

4. Click the **Format** down arrow, and choose the desired file format. Note that each file format has different options. For the purpose of this procedure, the file will be saved as a JPEG file.

5. Click **Save**. The format's option dialog box appears, if applicable.

6. Choose the desired options, and click **OK**.

7. Choose **File | Close** to close the image.

Chapter 8

Enhancing and Correcting Images

In the last chapter, you learned how to use Photoshop Elements to do some basic image editing. But wait, there's more! After you finish your basic editing, you can enhance a photo. In this chapter you'll learn to use Photoshop Elements tools and features to add pizzazz and presence to your photos.

Work with Layers

Photoshop Elements has a powerful feature known as layers. When you open an image in Photoshop Elements, you have one layer to work with, the background layer, which is the original image. You can add as many layers as you need on top of the background layer. Additional layers can be duplicates of the background layer, selections from other layers, adjustment layers, and so on. You can control what effect a layer has on underlying layers by choosing a blend

Figure 8-1: **You organize layers in the Layers palette.**

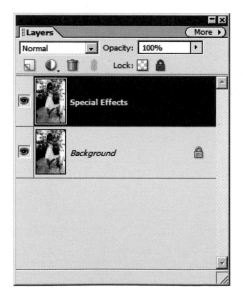

mode and varying the layer opacity. The beauty of working with layers is that you can duplicate the background layer and start editing the image on the layer. If the results are not pleasing, discard the duplicate layer, and you still have your original image with nary a pixel altered.

Create a Layer

You can create layers either using menu commands or from within the Layers palette. You modify layers from within the Layers palette. You can change the layer blend mode, vary opacity, change the order in which layers are stacked, and so on. When you work with layers, the top layer eclipses all layers beneath it. You can change the way the image looks by choosing a different blend mode for a layer. The blend mode determines how Photoshop Elements blends the pixels from the underlying layer with the pixels on the layer to which the blend mode is applied. You can also change the look of the top layer by varying layer opacity, which lets some of the underlying layer show through. Figure 8-1 shows the Layers palette of an image with several layers. For the purpose of this illustration, the Layers palette has been undocked from the Palette Bin.

Duplicate a Layer

When you apply menu commands or filters to an image, you destroy pixels. If you go too far, the image may be unusable and you'll have done a lot of work for nothing. However, if you duplicate the background layer and do all your work there, you still have the background layer as a fail-safe. Duplicating layers is also useful when you need to repair an underexposed or overexposed image.

1. Select the background layer in the Layers palette.

2. Drag the layer to the **Create A New Layer** icon to create a duplicate layer. Alternatively, you can choose **Layer I Duplicate Layer** or press CTRL+J (Windows) or COMMAND+J (Macintosh).

3. Double-click the default layer name, and type a new name for the layer. Naming layers is a good work habit when you're creating several layers to enhance an image.

TIP

TIP

You can change the order in which layers are stacked by dragging a selected layer above or below its current position. You cannot move the background layer until you unlock it by double-clicking the lock icon.

TIP

To undock a palette, click its name and drag it into the workspace. To redock a floating palette, click its name and drag it to the Palette Bin.

Choose Layer Blend Modes and Varying Opacity

You control the effect one layer has upon the underlying layer by choosing the desired blend mode. Photoshop Elements has a large variety of blend modes. Unfortunately, a detailed discussion of them is beyond the scope of this book. The following list describes a few modes commonly used when working with digital images:

- **Normal** is the default blending mode that displays the pixels on the layer in their original form without blending pixels from the underlying layer.

- **Multiply** effectively darkens the layer by multiplying the pixels on the layer by the pixels on the underlying layer, as shown in the following image.

- **Screen** effectively lightens the layer, except where the pixels are pure black, as shown in the following image.

- **Soft Light** darkens or lightens the pixels, depending on whether the underlying pixels are darker or lighter than midtone gray. The effect is similar to shining a diffused light on the image, as shown below.

The overall effect of the blended layers depends on the opacity you choose for each layer. By default, the opacity for each layer is 100 percent. If you choose a lower value, more of the pixels on the underlying layer show through.

Select a Blending Mode

1. Select the layer whose blending mode you want to change.

2. Click the down arrow to the right of the currently selected blend mode to reveal the Blend Mode drop-down list.

3. Click the desired blend mode to apply it.

Vary Layer Opacity

1. Select the layer whose opacity you want to change.

2. Click the down arrow to the right of the current layer opacity (100 percent, by default) to reveal the Opacity slider. Alternatively, you can move your cursor over the word "Opacity." When your cursor becomes a pointing finger with a horizontal two-headed arrow, drag left to decrease opacity or drag to the right to increase opacity.

3. Drag the slider to change the layer opacity.

4. Release the slider when the desired opacity has been achieved. Alternatively, you can type a value in the Opacity text field.

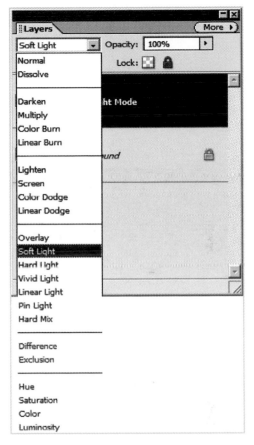

Use Adjustment Layers

You use adjustment layers to modify the image. The beauty of adjustment layers is that the original image is unchanged. The adjustment layer is pure mathematics that is applied to the image without changing the underlying layer. You can apply many of the same edits using menu commands. However, when you apply a menu command, the edit cannot be changed after you apply other commands. Conversely, you can edit an adjustment layer at any time to fine-tune the look of your image, or, for that matter, delete the adjustment layer if you don't like the effect.

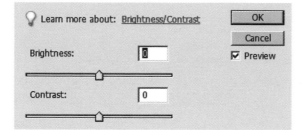

1. Select the layer you want to adjust.

2. Click the **Adjustment Layer** icon at the top of the Layers palette.

3. Select one of the adjustment layers from the drop-down menu. The rest of this procedure explains how to use some of the adjustment layers.

4. To change the brightness and/or contrast of the image, choose **Brightness/Contrast** from the drop-down menu to reveal the Brightness/Contrast dialog box. Then drag the Brightness and Contrast sliders to achieve the desired effect. As you drag the sliders, your image updates in real time.

5. Click **OK** to apply the brightness and/or contrast adjustment layer.

6. To change the hue and/or saturation of the image, choose **Hue/Saturation** from the drop-down menu to reveal the Hue/Saturation dialog box.

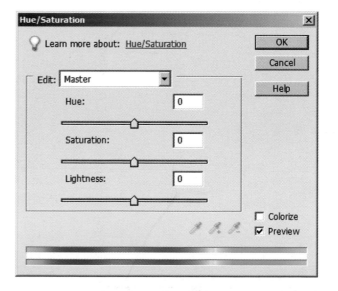

TIP

When you flatten layers, you can no longer edit them. Flattening layers is the final step when you're satisfied with the image.

TIP

If you don't like the results of an adjustment layer after further editing, you can change the adjustment layer settings by double-clicking the icon in the Layers palette. This reveals the dialog box for the adjustment layer, which makes it possible for you to alter the settings to your liking.

TIP

To delete any layer in the Layers palette, select it and drag it to the trashcan icon in the upper-left corner of the palette.

TIP

To create an image with a sepia-like tone, add a solid color adjustment layer to the image. Make sure this layer is at the top of the stack. Choose a reddish-brown color. Specify the **Color** blending mode, and lower the layer opacity until you create a reasonable facsimile of a sepia-type image.

UICKSTEPS

CREATING A VIGNETTE

One way you can enhance a portrait of a person is by adding a vignette. You can create your own custom vignette in Photoshop Elements through the use of layers and the Elliptical Marquee selection tool.

1. Open a portrait. A head-and-shoulders shot is perfect for this technique.

2. Select the background layer, and drag it to the **Create A New Layer** icon.

3. Rename the new layer "Vignette."

4. Select the **Elliptical Marquee** tool.

5. Create a selection around the desired section of the portrait. Remember, you can press the **SPACEBAR** to move the selection as you're creating it. To fine-tune the position of the selection, click inside the selection, and drag to the desired location.

Continued . . .

7. Drag the **Hue** slider to change the overall hue of the image. Drag the **Saturation** slider to saturate or desaturate the colors in the image. Drag the **Lightness** slider to change the lightness of the image.

8. To change the hue, saturation, or lightness for specific colors in the image, click the **Edit** down arrow, and choose the desired color range from the drop-down list.

Master	Ctrl+~
Reds	Ctrl+1
Yellows	Ctrl+2
Greens	Ctrl+3
Cyans	Ctrl+4
Blues	Ctrl+5
Magentas	Ctrl+6

9. Click **OK** to apply the Hue/Saturation adjustment layer.

10. Choose **Layer | Flatten Image**.

11. Save the image in the desired format.

THE PHOTOSHOP ELEMENTS TOOLBAR

The Photoshop Elements toolbar is conveniently docked on the left side of the interface. On it, you'll find tools that you can use to edit images. In the upcoming sections, you'll use some of these tools to create special effects and apply other edits to images. Covering every tool in the toolbar is beyond the scope of this book. In order to create as compact a toolbar as possible, the Photoshop Elements programmers keep similar tools on the same spot on the toolbar. For example, the Lasso tools are grouped together. When tools are grouped together, a triangle appears at the lower-right corner of the tool icon. Click the triangle to reveal all tools in the group. The last used tool is displayed on the tool icon. You can also float the toolbar in the workspace by clicking the perforation line above the top tool and then dragging the toolbar to the desired location. This illustration shows the Photoshop Elements toolbar.

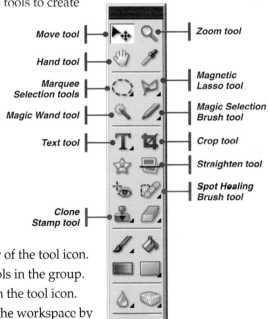

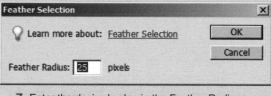

QUICKSTEPS

CREATING A VIGNETTE (Continued)

6. Choose **Select | Feather** to open the Feather
Selection dialog box. When you feather a
selection, you create a region where the pixels
inside the selection are gradually blended with
the pixels outside of the selection. This prevents
a hard edge from occurring around the selection,
which is ideal when you're using a layer to
segregate a special effect, such as a vignette.

Feather Selection	✕
💡 Learn more about: Feather Selection	OK
	Cancel
Feather Radius: 25 pixels	

7. Enter the desired value in the Feather Radius
field. This value is in pixels, and determines how
many pixels beyond the selection will be used for
the feather. The amount you enter depends on
the size of the image to which you're applying the
effect. If you're creating a vignette around a large
image, experiment with values 100 pixels or larger.

8. Click **OK** to apply the feather and close the
dialog box.

9. Choose **Select | Inverse**. This selects the area
where the vignette will be applied.

10. Choose **Edit | Fill Selection** to open the Fill Layer
dialog box.

11. Click the **Use** down arrow, and click **Black**.

12. Click **OK** to apply the fill.

Continued . . .

Fix a Photo with the Clone Tool

Sometimes, bad things happen to good photographs. For example, you may
have inadvertently grown a telephone pole out of your subject's head, or you
want to remove adults from pictures of your child's birthday party. You can fix
problems like this with the Clone tool.

1. Open the image that has an object you need to clone out.

2. Select the **Polygonal Lasso** tool, and create a selection around the object you need
to clone out, as shown here.

25.52%   © 8.533 inches x 6.4 inches (300 ppi) ▶ ◀

CREATING A VIGNETTE *(Continued)*

13. Select the **Vignette** layer, and drag the **Opacity** slider to 85 percent. Choose a higher value to reveal less of the underlying layer; choose a smaller value to reveal more. To see the effect the opacity has, click the eyeball icon on the background layer to momentarily hide the layer.

14. Choose **Select | Deselect** to remove the selection.

15. Click the **More** button in the Layers palette, and from the Layers menu, choose **Flatten Image**. This command flattens all the layers into the background layer in the image. Alternatively, you can choose **Layer | Flatten Image**. This step is not necessary if you're saving the file as a Photoshop *PSD file and you want the ability to edit layers at a future date. Your finished image should look something like the image to the right.

TIP

When you need maximum working space, press the **TAB** key to hide all palettes and tools that are floating in the workspace. When you do this, the currently selected tool is still active. Press the **TAB** key again to reveal the palettes and tools.

3. Select the **Clone** tool.

4. Size the brush. Press the right bracket ( ]) key to increase the size of the brush; press the left bracket key ([ ) to decrease the size of the brush.

5. Hold down the **ALT** key (Windows) or the **OPTION** key (Macintosh), and click the area in your photo from which you want to clone.

6. Drag inside the selection to clone out the offending object.

7. Choose **Select | Deselect** to remove the selection. The following illustration shows the previous photograph after the light poles have been cloned out of the yellow hot-rod's roof

TIP

You can also use the Clone tool to add elements to an image. For example, if you have a photograph of a person on grass that shows a few weeds, use the Clone tool to clone some green grass over the weeds.

QUICKSTEPS

CURING RED-EYE

If your digital camera does not have a red-eye reduction mode, when you take flash pictures of people, the flash reflects off their retinas and produces a red glow in the eyes. You can easily correct this problem in Photoshop Elements and return the person's eyes to normal.

1. Open the image of a subject that has red-eye.

2. Zoom in on the subject's eyes, as shown here.

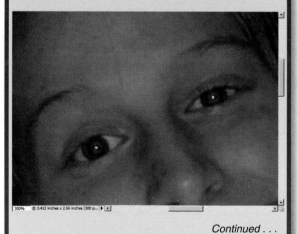

300%   © 3.413 inches x 2.56 inches (300 p...   ▶ ◀

Continued . . .

Touch Up Photos

Digital cameras are not perfect, and neither are photographers. Sometimes, camera and photographer are in synch, and the result is a wonderful photo. Then there are other times when Mother Nature fools the camera, or the photographer makes a wrong choice, and the result is a less-than-perfect photo. If that photo has redeeming value, you may be able to rescue it in Photoshop Elements. The following sections offer some remedies for common ailments.

Straighten a Photo

What seemed perfectly level when you looked at a scene through the viewfinder may not be once you get it into the computer for editing. Even professional photographers take photographs that aren't perfectly level. For example, picture an image of a sunset on the ocean with a horizon line that is not parallel with the top and bottom edges of the image. Fortunately, there's an easy fix for this problem.

1. Open an image where your subject is not level. In the case of the image shown here, the roof is not parallel with the top and bottom edges of the picture.

Straighten tool

25.15%   © 10.24 inches x 6.827 inches (300 ...   ▶ ◀

QUICKSTEPS

CURING RED-EYE *(Continued)*

3. Select the **Red-Eye Removal** tool.

4. Drag the tool over each eye. You may have to take a couple of swipes to remove all of the red-eye. The following image shows the subject's eyes after using the Red-Eye Removal tool.

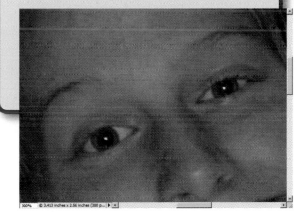

TIP

To use the Straighten tool on a vertical line, press **CTRL** (Windows) or **COMMAND** (Macintosh) while dragging the tool along a line that should be vertical.

TIP

You can have Photoshop Elements automatically crop the image by choosing **Crop To Remove Background** from the Canvas Options drop-down menu in the options bar.

2. Select the **Straighten** tool, and drag it along an edge that should be horizontal. When you release the mouse button, Photoshop Elements straightens the image.

3. Use the **Crop** tool to remove the white space at the edges of the image. The repaired image is shown in the following illustration.

Rescue Underexposed or Washed-Out Photos

If you have some dark, underexposed photos, you may be able to save them using the Shadows/Highlights command discussed in Chapter 7. You may also have some washed-out photos where the sky is too light. Don't discard these photos; you may be able to rescue them using layers and blending modes.

Rescue Washed-Out Images

1. Open an image that's overexposed or washed-out.

2. Open the **Layers** palette.

3. Select the background layer, and drag it to the **Create A New Layer** icon.

4. Select the new layer.

5. Change to the **Multiply** blending mode. This will give the image better contrast and detail.

6. If the image is now underexposed, lower the opacity of the layer.

Rescue Underexposed Images

1. Open an image that's underexposed.
2. Open the **Layers** palette.
3. Select the background layer, and drag it to the **Create A New Layer** icon.
4. Select the new layer.
5. Change to the **Screen** blending mode. The image is now brighter.

6. If the image is now too light, lower the opacity of the layer.

Convert an Image to Black and White

Digital cameras give you wonderful full-color images. However, sometimes things look better in black and white. For example, some portraits look stunning as black-and-white pictures.

ENHANCING A SUNSET

Sunsets make wonderful photographs. However, what looked perfect through the viewfinder may lack a little luster when you get the image into your computer. You can add life to a bland sunset by using an adjustment layer.

1. Open the image in Photoshop Elements.
2. Open the **Layers** palette.
3. Click the **Adjustment Layer** icon, and from the drop-down menu, choose **Photo Filter** to open the Photo Filter dialog box.
4. Choose one of the warming filters from the drop-down menu.
5. Drag the **Density** slider until you see something you like. A value of 50 percent works well in most instances.

Continued . . .

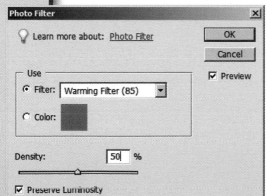

QUICKSTEPS

ENHANCING A SUNSET *(Continued)*

6. Click **OK** to apply the adjustment layer.

7. Choose **Layer | Flatten** and then save the image. The following is a photo enhanced with this technique. Notice the nice orange glow on the clouds.

Black-and-white images are also wonderful for landscapes that have a lot of contrast.

1. Open the image you want to convert to black and white.

2. Choose **Enhance | Convert To Black And White** to open the Convert To Black And White dialog box.

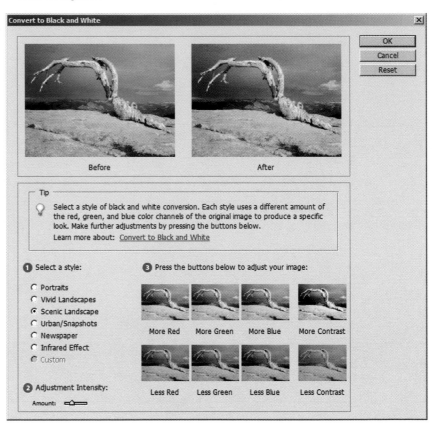

3. Choose one of the preset styles that suits the photo you're converting to black and white.

4. If desired, you can modify the preset by clicking one or more of the thumbnails. The thumbnails vary the percentage in each of the color channels. The image is still in the RGB (red, green, blue) color mode. You can also increase or decrease the contrast in the image. The Adjustment Intensity slider determines the amount of each adjustment. The default setting applies small amounts. Drag the slider to the right to increase intensity; drag to the left to decrease intensity.

5. Click **OK** to complete the conversion. The converted black-and-white image is shown in the following illustration.

Add Text to an Image

You can add text to any image you edit with Photoshop Elements. You can add text to an image that will become a greeting card, poster, or framed artwork. You can create vertical or horizontal text using any font currently installed on your system.

Create Text

1. Open the image to which you want to add text.

2. Select the **Text** tool.

TIP

To match a color in the image, move your cursor outside of the Color Picker. Your cursor becomes an eyedropper, signifying you can sample a color from within the image. Click the desired color to select it.

TIP

Photoshop Elements installs several Adobe Pro fonts with the application. Fonts such as Adobe Caslon Pro are particularly well suited for text on posters or cards.

TIP

You can align layers by selecting the **Move** tool and then, in the Layers palette, selecting the background layer and holding down the **SHIFT** key as you click the layers you want to align. In the options bar, choose an option from the Align drop-down menu.

3. In the options bar, click the **Vertical Text** or **Horizontal Text** icon.

4. Click the down arrow to the right of the currently selected font, and select the desired font family from the drop-down list.

5. Click the down arrow to the right of the currently selected font size, and choose an option from the drop-down list. Alternatively, you can type the desired value in the text field.

6. Click the desired alignment icon to left-align, center, or right-align the text.

7. Click the text color swatch to open the Color Picker.

8. Drag the arrows to the right of the **Color** slider to choose the hue, and drag inside the **Color** field to set the saturation.

9. Click **OK** to exit the Color Picker.

10. Click inside the document, and type the desired text. Photoshop Elements creates a layer for the text.

11. Click the **Commit** button (it looks like a check mark) in the Options bar.

12. Select the **Move** tool.

13. Drag the text to the desired location.

Add a Drop Shadow to Text

1. Open the **Layers** palette.

2. Select the text layer to which you want to apply the drop shadow.

3. In the Artwork And Effects palette, click the **Text** icon, as shown here.

4. Double-click the **Drop Shadow** icon. A gear icon appears on the layer, signifying that a style has been applied to the layer.

5. Double-click the gear icon to open the Style Settings dialog box. From within the dialog box, you can change the lighting angle, size, distance, and opacity as shown in the following illustration.

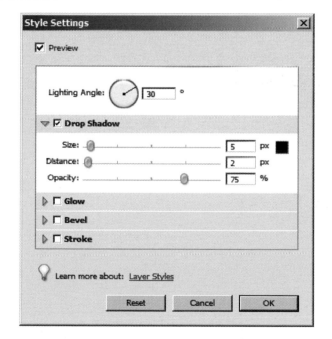

6. Click **OK** to apply the settings to the style. The image to the left shows text to which a drop shadow has been applied.

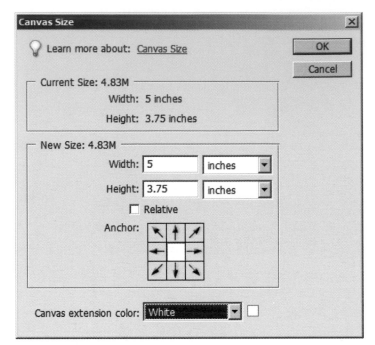

Add a Photo Border

It's easy to create a photo border around a digital image. When you display a photo with a border on a Web page with a contrasting background, it looks like an image in a scrapbook.

1. Open the image to which you want to add the photo border.

2. Choose **Image | Resize | Canvas Size** to open the Canvas Size dialog box.

3. Enter values for the Width and Height fields. The values you enter will be the current size of the image, plus the desired border dimension. If you're working with a 4 × 6 image, a border of 1/4 or 3/8 inch is a good choice. Alternatively, you can click the **Relative** check box, and then enter the desired value for the border.

4. From the Canvas Extension Color drop-down menu, choose **White**.

5. Click **OK** to add the border. This effect was applied to the following image.

Crop an Image Using the Rule of Thirds

Sometimes, you get your composition just right. But, other times in the heat of fire, you squeeze the shutter without thinking of composition. With a few simple steps, you can resize an image and get perfect composition at the same time.

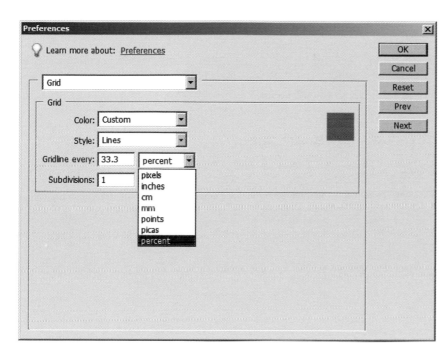

1. Choose **Edit | Preferences | Grid** to display the Grid section of the Preferences dialog box.

2. In the Gridline Every text box, type 33.3.

3. From the Gridline Every drop-down menu, choose **Percent**.

4. Click **OK** to close the Preferences dialog box.

5. Open the image you want to crop and recompose.

6. Choose **File | New | Blank File** to open the New dialog box.

7. Choose the desired image size from the Preset drop-down menu. Alternatively, you can enter values for width, height, and resolution. The image to the left shows the dialog box as configured for a 6 × 4-inch image with a resolution of 300 dpi. Remember to specify a size that is smaller than your original image. After all, you are cropping and changing the composition.

8. Click **OK** to create the blank document.

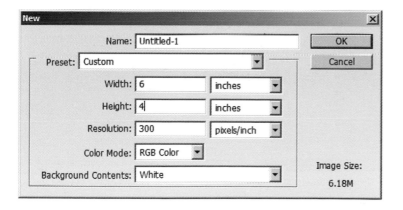

8

9. Choose **View | Grid**. The grid is displayed on the blank document. The gridlines are your guide for composing the image to the Rule of Thirds.

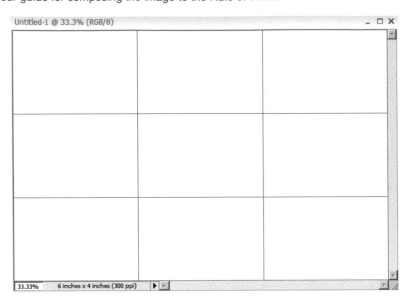

10. Select the original image, and then choose **Select | All**.

11. Choose **Edit | Copy** to copy the image to the Clipboard.

12. Position your cursor in the new document, and then choose **Edit | Paste**. Photoshop Elements pastes the image on a new layer.

13. Select the **Move** tool, and drag one of the corner handles. The layer resizing parameters appear on the options bar, as shown below. Click the **Constrain Proportions** check box, if it is not already selected.

14. Continue resizing and moving the layer. Your goal is to align an object with the intersection of two grid lines.

TIP

When using the Move tool, you can nudge a layer by one pixel with your keyboard arrow keys. Press **SHIFT** and an arrow key to nudge the layer by 10 pixels.

UNDERSTANDING THE UNDO HISTORY PALETTE

When you edit an image in Photoshop Elements, the application remembers the last 20 steps you've applied to the image. You can undo the last step by choosing **Edit I Undo**. You can undo additional steps by continuing to choose **Edit I Undo**, or redo the last undone step by choosing **Edit I Redo**. You can also manually select a step from within the Undo History palette. To access the Undo History palette (shown in the following illustration), choose **Window I Undo History**. In the Undo History palette, you can step backward and forward by dragging the right-pointing arrow on the left side of the palette or by clicking a History state. You can delete a selected step and all steps that were applied after it by selecting the step and then choosing **Delete** from the More menu. The Undo History palette tracks the last 20 steps you performed. If you're not satisfied with any of your edits, you can undo all steps by choosing **Edit I Revert**. If your system has enough resources, you can change the number of steps to a higher value by changing the History States value in the General Preferences dialog box (press **CTRL+K** in Windows or **COMMAND+K** in Macintosh).

15. Choose **Layer I Flatten Layers**, and then save the image in the desired file format. The following image shows a photo that has been cropped and recomposed using this technique. The setting sun was aligned to the intersection of two grid points to add interest to the image.

Retouch a Portrait

Digital cameras and modern lenses record every detail in an image. This is a good thing when you're photographing landscapes, but not so good when you're photographing someone with facial flaws, such as crow's feet. You can remove or reduce these features by implementing some techniques used by fashion and glamour photographers. Photoshop Elements has two wonderful tools for retouching images: the Healing Brush tool and the Spot Healing Brush tool.

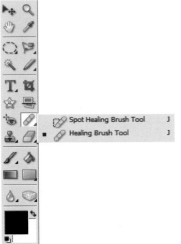

1. Open the image you want to retouch.

2. Examine the image and decide which areas you are going to retouch. The portrait to the right could stand some retouching around the eyes and the chin. To retouch areas such as crow's feet and lines under the eyes, the Healing Brush is the tool of choice.

3. Drag the background layer to the **Create A New Layer** icon in the Layers palette.

4. Select the **Healing Brush** tool.

5. Select the **Zoom** tool, and zoom in on the area you're retouching.

6. Hold down the **ALT** key (Windows) or the **OPTION** key (Macintosh), and click an area of unblemished skin that closely matches the texture of the area you're retouching.

7. Resize the tip of the Healing Brush tool so that it's slightly larger than the area you're retouching. Press the left bracket key ([ ) to decrease the size of the brush or the right bracket key ( ]) to increase the size of the brush.

8. Brush over the area you want to retouch. Photoshop Elements retouches the area using pixels from the area you sampled in step 6.

9. Continue sampling and retouching the photo. After you've retouched crow's feet and lines under the eyes, for example, you're ready to tackle flaws like freckles and pimples, which is a job for the Spot Healing Brush tool.

10. Select the **Spot Healing Brush** tool.

TIP

When retouching a photo, it's a good idea to do your work on a duplicate layer. If you're not pleased with the results, you can delete the layer to which you've applied the edits. Your original image is intact on the background layer.

TIP

The Healing Brush tool can also be used to restore old photos. For example, you can use the tool to repair a fold or tear in a photo that you've scanned into your computer.

11. Resize the tool so that it's slightly larger than the area you're retouching. Press the left bracket key ([ ) to decrease the size of the brush, or the right bracket key ( ]) to increase the size of the brush.

12. Click the area you want to retouch. Photoshop Elements replaces the spot with pixels from the surrounding area. After you've retouched the image, you may be tempted to save it. However, if you totally remove lines from a portrait of a middle-aged person or a senior citizen, the retouched image will look unnatural. The image to the left shows the portrait with the crow's feet, lines, and blemishes removed.

13. Lower the opacity of the retouch layer to display some of the underlying layer. The image to the right shows the retouched portrait with the retouch layer lowered to 65 percent opacity.

14. Choose **Layer | Flatten Image**, and then save the retouched photo in the desired format.

TIP

The Spot Healing Brush tool can be used to eliminate dust spots on images that appear because dust got onto your digital SLR camera sensor when changing lenses.

TIP

When you apply filters to an image, duplicate the background layer, and then apply the filter to the duplicated layer. You can then vary the effect by changing the opacity of the layer to which you apply the filter.

Add Panache with Filters

Photoshop Elements ships with a treasure trove of filters—more than you'll probably ever use. The following sections will show you how to use filters to add style to your images and create special effects. You can access filters from the Filter menu or from the Artwork And Effects palette, shown in Figure 8-2.

USING THIRD-PARTY FILTERS

In addition to using the filters that ship with Photoshop Elements, you can augment your work using third-party filters. Before you purchase third-party filters, however, make sure that they're compatible with Photoshop Elements. When you install these filters according to the manufacturer's instructions, most appear at the end of the Filters menu, while some appear in the Automation Tools menu. Four prominent filter manufacturers are Alien Skin Software (www.alienskin.com), Andromeda Software (www.andromeda.com), Auto FX (www.autofx .com), and Nik Software (www.niksoftware.com). The following image has been enhanced with the Monday Morning Sepia styling filter from Nik Software.

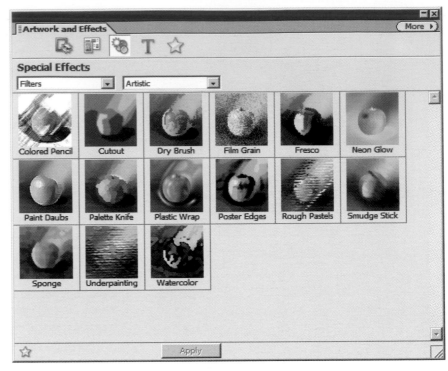

*Figure 8-2: **You can create special effects using filters on the Filter menu or from the Artwork And Effects palette.***

Create a Zoom Blur

One cool effect photographers use is to mount a camera on a tripod and select a small aperture (high f-stop number) to achieve a slow shutter speed. Then they take a picture of an object with their zoom lens at its lowest magnification and quickly zoom to the highest magnification. The effect makes it look as though the object is rushing toward you. You can achieve the same effect in Photoshop Elements using the Radial Blur filter.

1. Open the image to which you want to apply the zoom blur effect. The image to the left shows a perfect candidate for this effect: a photo of an exotic car. Unfortunately, the foliage and columns distract viewers from the car.

2. Choose **Filter I Blur I Radial Blur** to open the Radial Blur dialog box. Notice that this dialog box does not have a preview area.

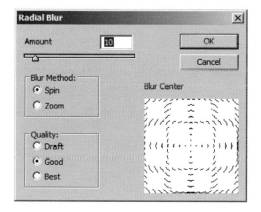

3. Drag the slider to the desired blur amount. A value between 10 and 15 works well for this effect.

4. In the Blur Method section, click the **Zoom** option.

5. In the Quality section, click the desired quality option. Choose **Best** for a high-quality image (at the expense of a longer render time).

6. Click **OK** to apply the effect. The image to the left shows the exotic car after the effect has been applied.

Simulate a Fish-Eye Lens

1. Open an image that you want to appear as though it was photographed with a fish-eye lens.

2. Select the **Crop** tool.

3. Click at the top of the image and, while holding down the **SHIFT** key, drag the tool to the bottom of the image. When you hold down the **SHIFT** key, you constrain the cropping box to a square, which is perfect for a fish-eye look.

4. Click the **Commit** button at the lower-right corner of the crop marquee (it looks like a check mark).

TIP

If you want part of the image to be unaffected by the filter, create a selection using the Elliptical Marquee tool. Invert the selection (choose **Select I Inverse**), feather the selection by an appropriate amount, and then apply the filter.

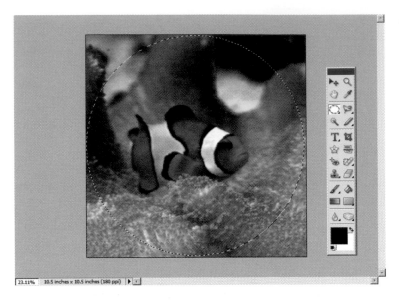

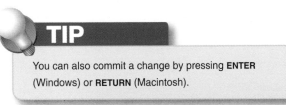

TIP

You can also commit a change by pressing **ENTER** (Windows) or **RETURN** (Macintosh).

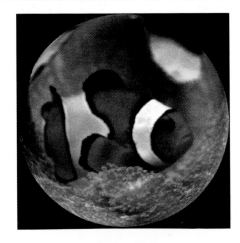

5. Select the **Elliptical Marquee** tool, and create a circular section that stretches from top to bottom and from side to side, as shown in the image to the left. Remember, to create a perfect circle, hold down the **SHIFT** key while dragging. Press the **SPACEBAR** momentarily to move the selection while creating it.

6. Choose **Filter | Distort | Spherize**.

7. Drag the **Amount** slider to 100, as shown below.

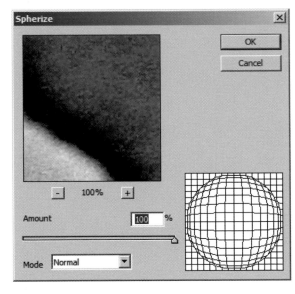

8. Click **OK** to apply the filter.

9. Choose **Select | Inverse**.

10. Choose **Edit | Fill** to open the Fill dialog box.

11. Click the **Use** down arrow, and choose **Black** from the drop-down menu.

12. Click **OK** to fill the selection.

13. Choose **Select | Deselect**. The illustration set to the left shows an image with this effect applied.

Chapter 9

Organizing Your Digital Image Library

When you start using your digital camera in earnest, you'll soon have many folders of images on your hard drive. If you followed the advice I presented in Chapter 7, your folders have logical names that make it easy for you to figure out what images are stored in what folder. In this chapter, you'll learn steps to further organize your digital image galleries and archive them to a CD or external hard drive.

Organize Your Digital Image Library

After several months of picture-taking, your hard drive may have hundreds or even thousands of images. If you employ good housekeeping and segregate similar image files into a named folder when you download them from your camera to the computer, you've taken the first step in organizing your photos. The Photoshop Elements Organizer workspace is your biggest ally when it comes to organizing your digital image library.

NOTE

As of this writing, the latest version of Photoshop Elements for the Macintosh is Version 4. Due to the fact that the Macintosh application iPhoto has an organizer, Adobe does not include an organizer with Photoshop Elements 4 for the Macintosh. Photoshop Elements 4 for Macintosh does have the Adobe Bridge 1.0, which can be used to perform certain organizing tasks. However, covering Adobe Bridge 1.0 is beyond the scope of this book.

Launch the Organizer Workspace

The Photoshop Elements Organizer workspace makes it possible for you to visually sift through your images. You can also add tags to images, which makes it easier to find the images you want. You can sort images and use the Organizer workspace timeline to view images by the date they were created.

1. Launch Photoshop Elements. The Photoshop Elements Welcome screen appears.

2. Click the **View And Organize Photos** icon. The Photoshop Elements Organizer workspace appears, as shown in Figure 9-1.

Figure 9-1: **You can view and organize your images with the Photoshop Elements Organizer.**

NOTE

All discussions on Photoshop Elements Organizer in this chapter refer to the Windows version of the application.

TIP

You can also launch the Organizer workspace by clicking the **Organize** icon within the Quick Fix or Full Edit workspaces.

TIP

By default, Photoshop Elements automatically imports images into the Organizer when you connect your camera or card reader. If you prefer to manually import images, choose **Edit Preference**. Click **Camera Or Card Reader**, and then clear the **Auto Launch Adobe Photo Downloader On Device Connect** option.

TIP

Clear the **Fix Red-Eye** option, unless you're importing folders with images of people that may contain red-eye, as this will speed up the import process. When the Fix Red-Eye option is enabled, Photoshop Elements looks for red-eye in every photo.

TIP

To prevent the information dialog box from appearing each time you import images, click the **Don't Show Again** check box.

Import Images

If you followed my suggestions in Chapter 7, you have a main folder for all of your digital images and it is divided into subfolders that contain images—these may have been photographed at a certain place, to be of a particular subject or person, or taken at a certain time. When the Photoshop Elements Organizer batch of images you viewed are displayed. To import images into the Organizer:

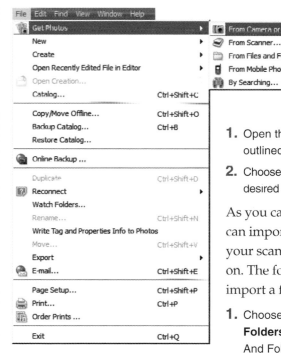

1. Open the Photoshop Elements Organizer, as outlined previously.

2. Choose **File | Get Photos**, and then choose the desired option from the submenu, as shown here.

As you can see from this illustration, you can import photos from a card reader, your scanner, from a mobile phone, and so on. The following steps show you how to import a folder of images.

1. Choose **File | Get Photos | From Files And Folders** to display the Get Photos From Files And Folders dialog box.

2. Navigate to the folder that contains the images you want to import. At this stage, you can click **Open** to open the folder and select individual images or click **Get Photos** to import the entire folder. You also have the option to import photos from subfolders and to automatically fix red-eye, if detected. These options are selected by default. After you import photos, a dialog box appears, telling you that the items in the main window are the ones you just imported.

3. Click **Back To All Photos** to view your entire catalog.

View Images in the Organizer

When you open the Organizer, the last images you viewed appear in the main window. You can control the size of thumbnails, view single images, or watch a slide show in Full Screen mode. When you display images as thumbnails, you have the equivalent of a digital light box.

Change Organizer View

You can change the thumbnail size at any time. Doing this enables you to view more thumbnails at one time when you select a small thumbnail size or more image details when you choose a larger thumbnail size. You can also display single images in the main window or view images in Full Screen mode.

1. Open the Photoshop Elements Organizer workspace, as outlined previously. This illustration shows the main window of the Organizer.

2. Drag the **Timeline** slider to view images photographed during a certain month and year. Each year is marked on the timeline, with vertical marks that indicate the relative amount of photos created during each month. Taller marks mean more images were created on that month. You can also hold your cursor over a vertical mark to see the month as a tooltip.

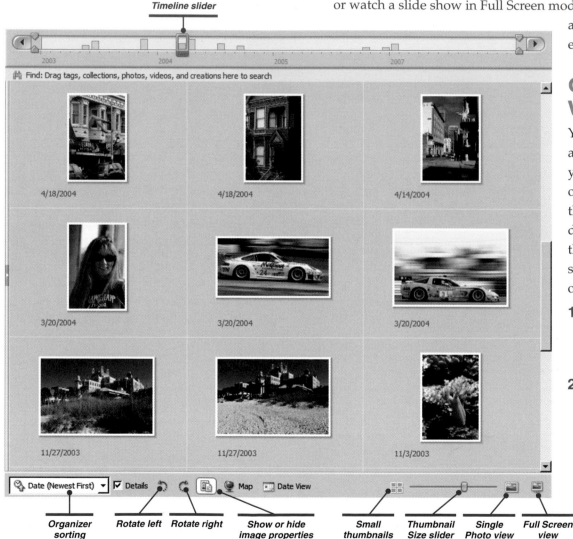

Timeline slider

Organizer sorting *Rotate left* *Rotate right* *Show or hide image properties* *Small thumbnails* *Thumbnail Size slider* *Single Photo view* *Full Screen view*

3. Click the **Details** check box (it is selected by default) to prevent image details from being displayed under each thumbnail.

4. Click the **Date** icon to view images that were added to the Organizer by date. You can choose to view by year, in which case dates on which images were added to the Organizer are solid in color; by Month, in which case the last image that was imported on a given date appears on that date; or by Day, in which case the last image imported on a given day appears in the main window, along with thumbnails of other images imported on that date. When you view images by month or year, a player appears in the upper-right corner of the workspace, which enables you to see the next or previous image, as well as to play a slide show. The selected date is listed in the upper right corner of the workspace, along with arrows to advance to the next or previous day. The following image shows the Organizer workspace in the Month view.

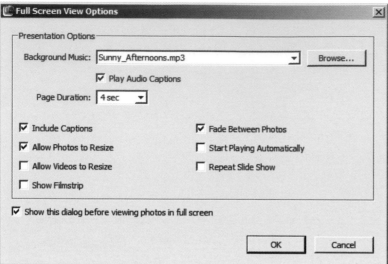

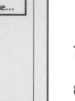

5. Click **Photo Browser** to view images as thumbnails.

6. Click the **Small Thumbnail Size** icon to display thumbnails at their smallest size. This option is convenient when you've imported a large batch of photos on a given date and want to view as many as possible.

7. Drag the **Thumbnail Size** slider to the right to increase the size of image thumbnails, or drag it to the left to decrease the size.

8. Click the **Single Photo** view to display just one image. When you choose this viewing option, a scrollbar appears on the right side of the main window, which enables you to view other photos imported on the same day.

9. Click the **Full Screen** view to display a single image on screen. When you choose this option, the Full Screen View Options dialog box appears, as shown here.

10. After choosing your options, click **OK** and press the SPACEBAR to begin viewing images in Full Screen mode.

11. Press ESC to return to the previous view.

TIP

To edit an image, select the image thumbnail, and then click **Edit** to reveal the Edit drop-down menu, which gives you the option of editing the image in Quick Fix or Full Edit mode.

View Image Properties

If you require more information than the thumbnail image offers, you can view the properties associated with the image, such as the date it was created, any tags that have been applied to the image, the date the image was modified and imported, as well as the Camera EXIF (Exchangeable Image File Format) information. The EXIF information gives the model of the camera used to photograph the image, exposure information, and the focal length. Viewing image properties is handy when you need to know information about a file, such as the file size, date created, or date modified, before opening it.

1. Open the Photoshop Elements Organizer workspace, as outlined previously.

2. Select a thumbnail.

3. Click the **Show/Hide Properties** icon at the bottom of the main window. Alternatively, you can press ALT+ENTER.

4. Click the applicable icon to view general properties, tags, history, or EXIF data. The image to the left shows the Properties palette as configured when viewing EXIF data.

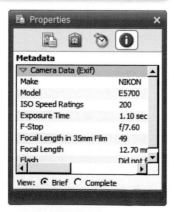

QUICKSTEPS

DELETING IMAGES

After you download images to your computer and view the thumbnails in the Organizer, you'll see some that are obvious candidates for deletion. You can easily delete one or more files from the Organizer.

1. Select the thumbnails of the images you want to delete.

2. Choose **Edit | Delete Selected Items From Catalog**. The Confirm Deletion From Catalog dialog box appears.

Confirm Deletion from Catalog

 The selected item(s) will be deleted from the catalog.

☐ Also delete selected item(s) from the hard disk

[OK] [Cancel]

---

3. Click the **Also Delete Selected Item(s) From The Hard Disk** check box to delete the images from both the catalog and your computer.

4. Click **OK** to delete the selected thumbnails from the catalog and, if specified, the hard drive.

Rotate Images

If your camera does not have an option to rotate images, pictures that were photographed with a vertical composition will be displayed horizontally in the File Browser. You can rotate images as needed so that they display properly in the File Browser.

1. Open the Photoshop Elements Organizer workspace, as outlined previously.

2. Select a thumbnail that is not oriented properly.

3. Click the **Rotate Left** or **Rotate Right** icon.

Sort Images

By default, the File Browser sorts all images by date, with the newest images appearing at the top of the main Organizer window. You can, however, change the manner in which files are sorted. You can sort files with the oldest images at the top of the main Organizer window, or you can display batches of images sorted by the date and time on which they were imported.

1. Click the **Organizer View** drop-down list at the lower-left corner of the Organizer workspace.

2. Choose one of the following options:

- **Date (Newest)** displays the newest images at the top of the main Organizer window.
- **Date (Oldest)** displays the oldest images at the top of the main Organizer window.
- **Import Batch** sorts images by the date and time on which they were imported. You can navigate from batch to batch using the Timeline slider at the top of the window or the scrollbars.
- **Folder Location** displays a folder tree on the left side of the workspace. Navigate to a folder, and then right-click to reveal a shortcut menu, with options that include adding unmanaged files to the catalog.

Batch-Process Image Files

You use the Photoshop Elements Batch Processing command to convert files from one file type to another. This option is especially useful if you have a

QUICKSTEPS

RENAMING YOUR DIGITAL IMAGES

When you take a picture with your digital camera, the camera creates a file name for the image. The file name contains a prefix (determined by the camera manufacturer) followed by a number. Unfortunately, the file name doesn't give you a clue about the image. You can use the Organizer to rename every digital image it contains. For example, if you have a folder filled with JPEG images from your vacation to Disneyland, you can rename the files Disney-1.jpg, Disney-2.jpg, and so on.

1. Open the Photoshop Elements Organizer workspace, as outlined previously.

2. Select the files you want to rename by clicking their thumbnails. You can select contiguous files by holding down the **SHIFT** key and clicking the first and last thumbnails of the files you want to rename. You can select noncontiguous files by holding down the **CTRL** key (Windows) or the **COMMAND** key (Macintosh) and clicking each file you want to select.

3. Choose **File | Rename**. The Rename dialog box appears.

4. Enter a name and click **OK**. Photoshop Elements renames the selected images with the specified name appended by -1, -2, etc.

folder of high-resolution files that you want to resize and save in a different file format. When you batch-process files, you can also rename the files, resize them, specify a different destination folder, and so on.

1. Launch Photoshop Elements and switch to Full Edit or Quick Fix mode.

2. Choose **File | Process Multiple Files** to open the Process Multiple Files dialog box.

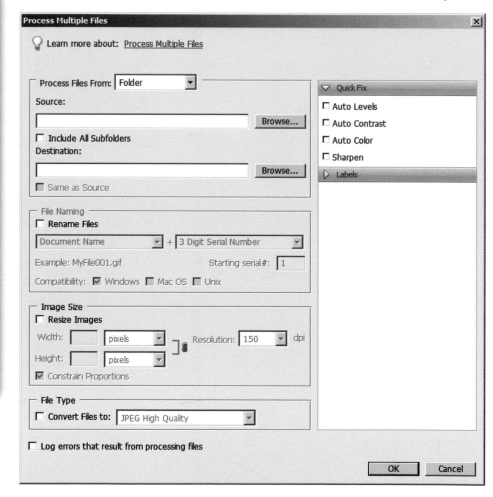

TIP

To avoid overwriting the original files, it's a good idea to save the processed files in a different folder. If you are saving the processed files in the same folder, make sure you rename them as outlined in step 6.

TIP

You can also batch-process files currently open in Photoshop Elements.

TIP

Do not enter a value for width or height that is larger than the dimensions of the files you are converting. If you enter a larger dimension, Photoshop Elements has to increase the size of pixels to the new image size at the current resolution, and image degradation will result.

TIP

You can also add a caption or watermark to images you process by clicking the right-pointing arrow and choosing **Watermark** or **Caption** from the drop-down menu. You can also choose to add a watermark or caption to every image processed.

3. Choose one of the following options from the Process Files drop-down menu:
   - **Folder** enables you to process the files in the folder you specify.
   - **Import** enables you to process files you import from a digital camera, card reader, or scanner attached to your computer.
   - **Open Files** enables you to process files currently open in Photoshop Elements.

4. Click **Include All Subfolders** to process images in subfolders of the selected folder.

5. In the Destination section, click **Browse** and navigate to the folder in which you want to save the processed files. Alternatively, you can click **Same As Source**, which saves the images in the same folder as the source images.

6. Click the **Rename Files** check box to rename the images you're processing, and then choose an option from the drop-down lists. For example, you can use the name of the photographed person or the place the images were taken, followed by the original file name or a serial number.

7. Choose compatibility options. By default, the images are compatible with the native operating system. You can also choose to make the images compatible with different operating systems, which is a handy feature if you're sharing photos with people whose computers use a different operating system from yours. Your compatibility options are Windows, Mac OS, and Unix.

8. Click the **Resize** check box to resize the images you're processing. Enter a value in the Width or Height field and accept the default **Constrain Proportions** option. Photoshop Elements will resize the image using the same proportions as the original image.

9. Choose an option from the Unit Of Measure drop-down menu.

10. Choose an option from the Resolution drop-down menu.

11. To convert the images to another file format, click the **Convert Files To** check box, and then choose the desired file type from the drop-down menu.

12. If desired, choose any of the Quick Fix options by clicking the applicable check boxes in the Quick Fix section of the dialog box.

13. Click **OK** to batch-process the images.

Add Tags to Images

When you end up with hundreds or even thousands of images on your hard drive, finding the photo you want to print or edit is like looking for a needle in a haystack. Fortunately, you can add tags to your images. Tags can be used as criteria when you're searching for a file. To add tags to an image:

1. Open the Photoshop Elements Organizer workspace, as outlined previously.

2. Choose **Window | Organize Bin**. The Organize Bin is displayed on the right side of the Organizer workspace, as shown here. Notice that the Organize Bin has several categories. You can add tags to these categories and apply them to images.

3. Click the **Tags** icon if the Tags section of the Organize Bin is not already displayed.

To create a new tag:

1. Select the desired category. For example, if you wanted to tag vacation photos, Places would be a good category in which to place the tag.

2. Click the **New** icon, and choose **New Tag** from the drop-down menu. Alternatively, you can press **CTRL+N** (Windows) or **COMMAND+N** (Macintosh). The Create Tag dialog box shown on the left appears.

3. Enter the name for the tag.

4. Click **OK**.

To add a tag to an image:

1. Open the Organize Bin, as outlined previously.

2. Drag the desired tag onto an image. You can add as many tags to an image as you want. You can also select multiple images and then apply the desired tag to all of them.

TIP

You can also create tag categories by choosing **New Category** from the New Tag menu and create sub-categories by choosing **New Sub Category** from the New Tag menu.

Create Tag

0 tagged items

Edit Icon...

Category: Places

Name:

Location: Not Located

Place on Map...

Note:

OK   Cancel

Create a Collection

Creating a collection is a wonderful way to segregate similar photos. When you create a collection, an icon is added to the Collections section of the Organize Bin. To create a collection:

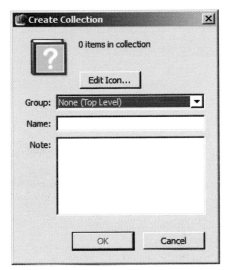

1. Open the Organizer workspace, and choose **Window I Organize Bin** to open the Organize Bin.

2. Click the **Collections** icon.

3. Choose **New Collection** from the New drop-down menu to display the Create Collection dialog box shown here.

4. Enter a name for the collection. If desired, you can add comments in the Notes section. Notes are not displayed in the Organizer workspace, but are visible when you edit the collection.

5. Click **OK**. Photoshop Elements adds an icon with the collection name to the Collections tab of the Organize Bin.

6. Drag the collection icon onto images to add them to the collection. Photoshop Elements creates the collection and uses the first image in the collection for the icon that appears in the Organize Bin. The image to the right shows a few collections in the Collections tab of the Organize Bin.

7. To display a collection, click the box to the left of the collection icon. A binoculars icon appears in the box, and the images in the collection are displayed.

TIP

You can create a selection of the images you want to add to a collection by holding down the **CTRL** key, clicking the desired images, and then dropping the desired collection icon on the photos.

TIP

You can choose one of the commands from the Find menu to find photos you want to add to a collection. After Photoshop Elements finds the photos that match your criteria, choose **Edit I Select All**, and then drag a collection icon onto one of the photos to add them all to the collection.

QUICKSTEPS

CREATING FOLDERS FOR CD ARCHIVES

When you archive images to a CD, you can create a folder for each disc. If you create contact sheets for your image folders, you'll have a handy cross-reference.

1. Create a new folder.

2. Rename the folder. A logical naming sequence would be Images_001, Images_002, and so on.

3. Drag the image folders you want to archive to the folder you just created.

8. To edit a collection, right-click a collection title, and then choose **Edit <*the name of the collection*>** from the context menu. This opens the Edit Collection dialog box, as shown here.

9. Click **Edit Icon** to change the collection icon. This opens the Edit Collection Icon dialog box, which enables you to crop the collection icon or choose a different icon from the images in the collection. Alternatively, you can click **Import**, which enables you to import an image not in the collection and use it for the collection icon.

Create a Contact Sheet

When you've got hundreds of images stored on your hard drive, you can use the Organizer to view a thumbnail image of the file before opening it. However, when you run low on hard disk space and save your files to CDs before deleting them from the hard drive, you'll have to pop each disc in the CD drive and then search for the desired files with the Organizer—a tedious task at best. Fortunately, there is a better way. You can create a contact sheet for the images you store on CDs. A contact sheet is a printed page that shows thumbnail-size pictures of image files. You can then store printed contact sheets in a loose-leaf binder for future reference.

1. Open the Organizer workspace, as outlined previously.

2. Select the photos for the contact sheet.

3. Choose **File I Print** to display the Print Photos dialog box.

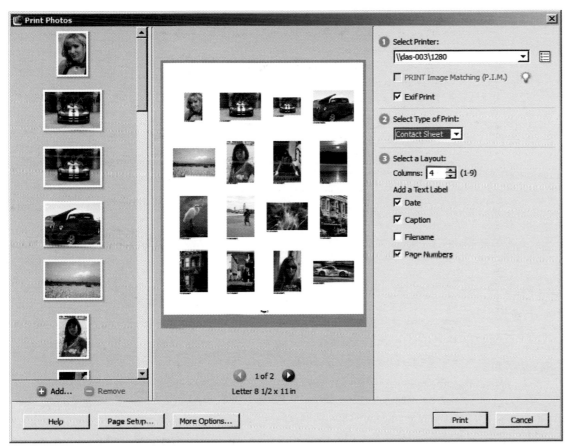

4. Choose **Contact Sheet** from the Select Type Of Print drop-down menu. The Print Photos box reconfigures, as shown here.

5. Choose the number of columns by entering a value in the text box or clicking the spinner.

6. Choose what you want to display on a text label. Note that if you add a text label and choose all of the relevant options, the text will be small and hard to read.

7. Click **Page Setup** and follow the prompts to choose the paper size and orientation options. You can also set up your printer from within this dialog box.

8. Click **OK** to exit the Page Setup dialog box.

9. Click **Print**. Photoshop Elements prints the contact sheets.

Archive Your Images

TIP

Don't use a regular marker to write on the CD disc. Regular markers can bleed through and damage your data. You can find CD- and DVD-safe markers at your local office supply store.

In a perfect world, computers would operate flawlessly and hard drives would last forever. Unfortunately, neither event occurs. Computers will crash when you least expect them to, and if they crash hard, they're liable to corrupt some of your files. To protect against this, you should always archive your digital images, and archive them frequently. That way, if the worst-case scenario happens, you have backups of your digital images. CD discs are dirt-cheap. Some people may think it's more logical to archive files

QUICKFACTS

TRANSFERRING FILES WITH REMOVABLE FLASH DRIVES

You can use a removable flash USB drive to transfer photos from one computer to another. These devices plug into a USB port and have capacities as high as 4 GB. Transfer the files from your computer to your removable flash drive. After safely removing the device from your system, you can connect it to a USB port on another computer and transfer your files. The image to the right shows a 1-GB removable flash drive.

to a DVD disc, but neither CDs nor DVDs are infallible. If a DVD disc is damaged, you lose almost 5 gigabytes (GB) of images. If a CD disc goes bad, you lose only 700 megabytes (MB) of images.

Archive Images

After you've created contact sheets and copied the image folders you want to archive to different folders, you're ready to archive the files to a CD. Windows and Macintosh operating systems both have built-in CD burning applications. Alternatively, you can purchase a third-party application, such as Nero (Windows) or Toast (Macintosh).

Back Up Image Files to an External Hard Drive

If you use your computer a lot, your hard drive takes a beating. Every time you launch a program or open a file, your computer's faithful servant, the hard drive, spins, locates, and serves up the required information. Like any mechanical device, a hard drive is subject to failure, and they will fail when you least expect them to. If you're fortunate, you may be able to recover the data from the crashed hard drive. Rather than suffer the loss of your image gallery when a hard drive crashes, you can be proactive and back up your files to an external hard drive. You can purchase an external 80-GB hard drive for as little as $150 at your local computer retail outlet, which is cheap insurance compared to the loss of your prized digital images.

Most external hard drives plug into an external AC adapter and connect to a (Universal Serial Bus) USB or FireWire port. Some external hard drives have ports to connect to both USB and FireWire. After you connect the device to a USB or FireWire port, your computer recognizes the device and you can copy files to the hard drive. If you get in the habit of copying all updated folders to the device once a week, you'll always have a backup of your digital images and other important information.

How to...

- Create a Picture Package
- Create a Contact Book
- Send Images via E-Mail
- Resize Images and Use the Save For Web Command
- Create a Web Photo Gallery
- Create a Virtual Slide Show
- Creating a Calendar
- Ordering Prints Online
- Create a Flip Book
- Print Your Photos After Previewing Them
- Choosing the Right Paper
- Investigating Alternative Papers

Chapter 10
Sharing Your Digital Photographs

After editing your images, you're ready to share them—whether with the world or a few close friends. With Photoshop Elements you can create picture packages, optimize images for the Web, create Web photo galleries, and more. Most of the features discussed in this chapter are only applicable to the Windows version of Photoshop Elements. Macintosh users can perform similar tasks using iPhoto. Unfortunately, a discussion of iPhoto is beyond the scope of this book.

Share Your Digital Images

There are so many ways you can share digital images with friends and family. You can create a picture package in Photoshop Elements that combines several sizes of the same image on one sheet of paper. You can also use the application to create slide shows, greeting cards, and more.

Create a Picture Package

When you create a picture package in Photoshop Elements, you can choose from several different layout options. For example, you can create a picture package that combines two 5 × 7 photographs on a single page or a picture package that combines one 5 × 7 and two 3 × 5 photographs on a single page. After you choose the layout, Photoshop Elements does its magic and creates the picture package, which you can then print.

1. Open the Organizer workspace, and then choose the image you want to print.

2. Choose **File | Print** to open the Print Photos dialog box.

3. Choose the desired printer from the Select Printer drop-down list.

4. Choose **Picture Package** from the Select Type Of Print drop-down list. At this stage, the image is shown in the default layout.

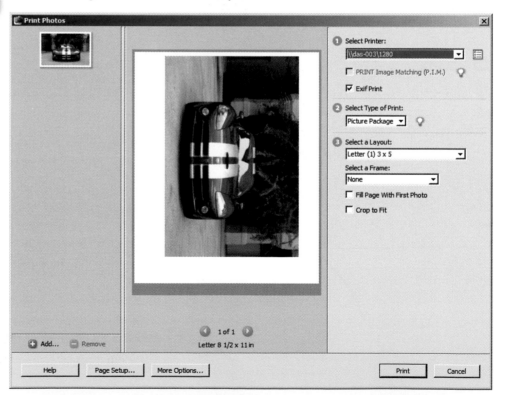

5. Choose an option from the Select A Layout drop-down list, shown in this illustration.

6. If desired, choose a frame from the Frame drop-down list.

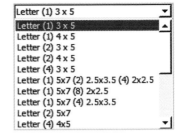

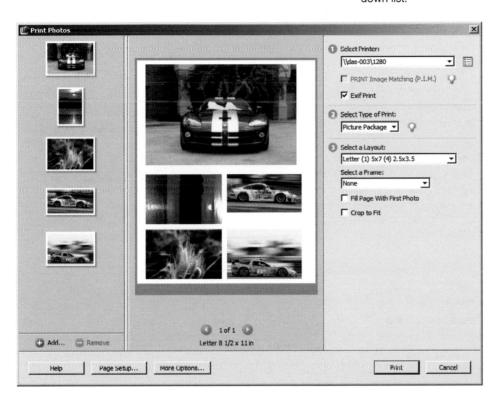

7. Click **Fill Page With First Photo** to create a picture package with the image you selected in step 1. Alternatively, you can click the **Add** button and choose enough photos to fill the available slots. Photoshop Elements fills the slots with pictures, as shown in the illustration to the left. If you're not satisfied with the layout, drag a photo from the left side of the dialog box, and drop it on top of the photo you want to replace.

8. Click **Crop To Fit**, and Photoshop Elements will crop the pictures to fit the layout perfectly.

9. Click **More Options** to open the More Options dialog box, which enables you to choose a color space with which the images are printed. Unless you've changed the profile in your camera or within Photoshop Elements, this step is not needed. If you have changed the color profile, choose **sRGBIEC6 1966-2.1** to print the image on an inkjet printer.

10. Click **Print** to print the picture package.

Share Your Images via E-mail

You can share any image in the Organizer with a friend via e-mail. When you share images, you can send them as attachments, in the body of the e-mail, or as PDF slide shows. You create a contact book in Photoshop Elements that you can then use for sending images and other creations to friends and colleagues via e-mail.

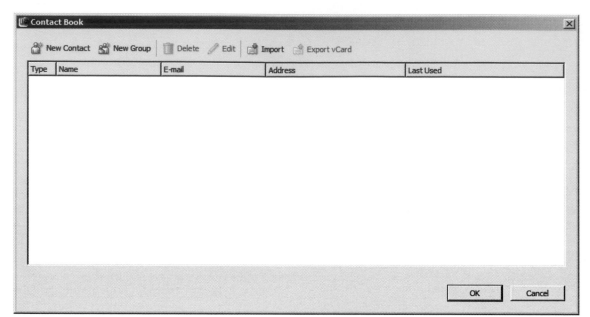

Create a Contact Book

You can create a contact book in Photoshop Elements that contains the e-mail addresses of friends and relatives. To create a contact book in Photoshop Elements:

1. In the Organizer workspace, choose **Edit | Contact Book** to open the Contact Book dialog box, as shown here.

2. Click **New Contact** to open the New Contact dialog box as shown below.

TIP

If you have a lot of contacts, you can organize them by contact groups. For example, you can keep friends in one contact group, relatives in another, and business associates in yet another. In the Contact Book dialog box, click **New Contact Group**, and follow the prompts to create a contact group to which you can add individual contacts.

TIP

If a member of your contact book's information changes, you can update it by opening the Contact Book dialog box, selecting the contact, and then clicking the **Edit** icon.

TIP

You can also send images that are open in the Full Edit or Quick Fix workspaces by clicking the icon that looks like a globe and envelope and choosing **E-mail**.

3. Fill in the fields to add a contact to your contact book.

4. Click **OK** to add the new entry to your contact book.

5. Click **OK** to close the Contact Book dialog box.

Send Images via E-mail

You can send images from the Organizer via e-mail. When you choose this option, Photoshop Elements automatically optimizes the images for e-mail delivery. As mentioned, you can send images as attachments, in the body of an e-mail message, or as a PDF document. To send images via e-mail:

1. In the Organizer workspace, select the images you want to send.

2. Choose **File | E-mail** to open the **Attach To E-mail** dialog box, as shown below. Alternatively, you can click the icon that looks like a globe and envelope, and then choose **E mail**.

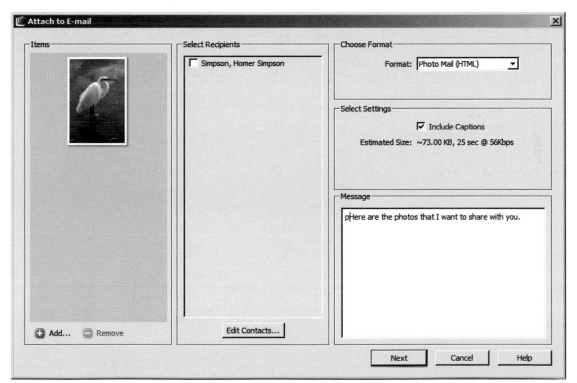

3. Click the check box of the recipients to whom you want to send the images.

4. Choose the manner in which you want to send the images from the Format drop-down list:

- **Photo Mail (HTML)** embeds the images in the body of the e-mail message.
- **Simple Slide Show (PDF)** creates a PDF slide show and attaches it to the e-mail.
- **Individual Attachments** sends the images as attached files.

If you choose the first option, go to step 5; otherwise, go to step 6.

5. Clear the **Include Captions** check box. If you accept this default option, Photoshop Elements will include captions with the images, provided the images have them. This option is only available when you embed images in the body of an e-mail.

6. If you send images as slide shows or attachments, the dialog box reconfigures accordingly. If you send images as slide shows, you're prompted to include a file name and specify an image size and quality, as shown above. If you send images as attachments, you need to specify image size and quality. Note that the large image sizes and high quality will increase file size and the amount of time it takes your recipient to download the message.

7. Accept the default message, modify, or change it. The remaining steps in this procedure show how to send embedded images in the body of an e-mail.

8. Click **Next** to open the Stationery & Layouts Wizard.

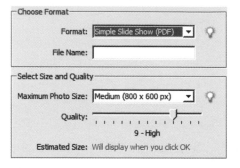

9. Choose the desired stationery, and then click **Next Step**. The Step 2: Customize The Layout page appears. Here you can change the image size, text, borders, and other options.

You may not be able to use Photoshop Elements to send messages via e-mail with some e-mail applications. If you find this to be the case with your e-mail application, follow the instructions in "Resize Images and Use the Save For Web Command."

10. Customize the layout and then click **Next**. Photoshop Elements opens your default e-mail application.

11. Send the message.

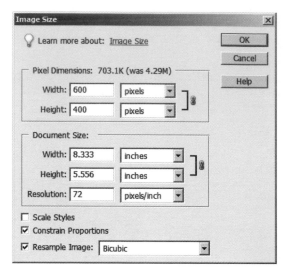

Resize Images and Use the Save For Web Command

If you want to post an image on a Web site, or if the e-mail option won't work with your e-mail application, you can resize high-resolution images and optimize them using the Save For Web command.

1. Open the image you want to resize and optimize in the Full Edit workspace.

2. Choose **Image | Resize | Image Size** to open the Image Size dialog box.

3. Resize the image so that the largest dimension is 640 pixels or less, and resample the image to 72 ppi, the resolution of a computer monitor. The illustration to the left shows an image being resized for a Web site.

4. Click **OK** to resize the image.

5. Choose **File | Save For Web** to open the Save For Web dialog box.

6. Choose **JPEG** from the Format drop-down list.

7. Click the **Quality** triangle, and then drag the slider to the left. This compresses the image to a smaller file size. As you drag the slider, look at the image in the window on the right. When you notice that the image quality is starting to degrade, drag the slider to the right. Alternatively, you can choose an option from the Compression Quality drop-down list.

8. Click **OK**. The Save As Optimized dialog box appears.

9. Enter a name for the image, and specify the location in which the image will be saved.

10. Click **Save**.

TIP

When saving an image for the web, don't have spaces in the filename as some web browsers don't treat spaces properly, which may cause the image not to load. If you must differentiate between words in a filename, use an underscore, or capitalize the first letter of the second word. For example, my_car.jpeg or myCar.jpeg.

Display Your Images on a Web Site

Many Internet service providers (ISPs) offer free Web sites to their customers, while others offer Web-hosting services at discounted prices. Today, it's easier than ever to create your own Web site. Your ISP may even provide you with ready-built templates for creating one. The following section shows you how to create a Web photo gallery.

Create a Web Photo Gallery

If you're not a Web design guru, don't worry—you can use Photoshop Elements to create a Web photo gallery. This features neatly arranged thumbnails of the images you want to display. When clicked, the thumbnail reveals a full-size image. Now, how cool is that?

1. Select the images you want to use in your Web gallery in the Organizer workspace.

2. Choose **Photo Galleries** from the Create drop-down list to display the Photoshop Elements Photo Galleries Wizard.

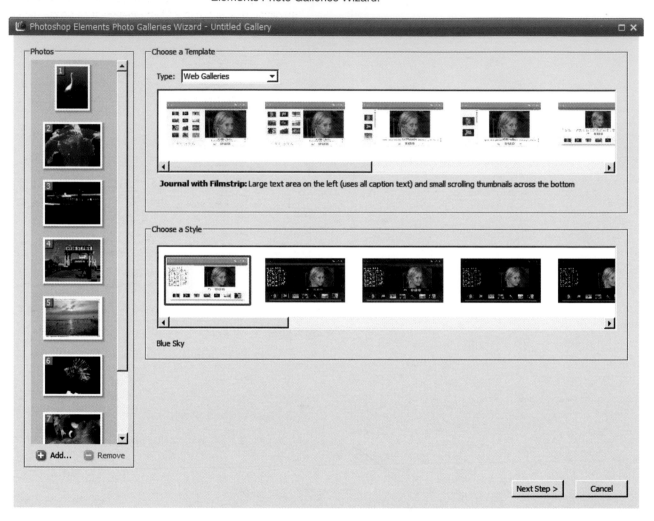

3. Choose an option from the Type drop-down list. Your options are Web Galleries, Animated, or Interactive.

4. Choose a template from the top row of thumbnails, and then choose a style from the second row of thumbnails.

5. Click **Next Step**. The Building Creation section of the wizard appears, and then the Photoshop Elements Photo Galleries Wizard reconfigures, as shown. In this section of the dialog box, you can add information such as the gallery title (which appears in the title bar of the Web browser in which the gallery is displayed), a gallery caption, your name and e-mail address, and so on. You can also modify the duration of each slide (if the template features a slide show), the slide show transition, and the colors and fonts used for the Web page. You can also specify the type of connection for which the gallery is optimized: Broadband (large images) or Dial-Up (medium images).

If you save the gallery to CD, make sure you choose label the CD with a CD marker. Otherwise, the ink of a regular marker may bleed through and damage the disc data. You can purchase markers that are safe for labeling CDs at your local office supply store.

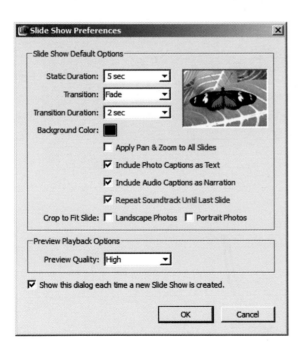

6. In the Browse And Share section, enter the name for the gallery and the location on your computer in which the gallery is saved.

7. Choose an option from the Share drop-down list. Your choices are Photoshop Showcase, My FTP Site, CD, or Do Not Share. Your next step depends on the option you choose. If you decide to share the gallery with the Photoshop Showcase (Photoshop Online Services), click **Upload** to upload the gallery. If you choose to share it on your FTP site, you're prompted for your FTP server, user name, password, and so on. If you choose CD and your CD-RW drive contains a blank CD, Photoshop Elements burns the gallery to CD; otherwise, you're prompted to insert a blank CD. If you choose Do Not Share, you save the gallery to the location specified in the Save To box. The saved gallery is listed in the Organizer, which you can share at a future date. Figure 10-1 shows a gallery as displayed in Internet Explorer.

Create a Virtual Slide Show

You can use Photoshop Elements to create a virtual slide show. The results can then be viewed by anyone who has the free Acrobat Reader or Windows Media Player installed on their computer. You can choose from many different styles, add background music to the slide show, and more.

1. Open the Organizer workspace, and select the images for your slide show.

2. Choose **Slide Show** from the Create drop-down list to display the Slide Show Preferences dialog box.

3. Specify the static duration, type of transition, and duration of the transition.

4. Choose the background color, whether or not to apply pan and zoom to each slide, caption options, and soundtrack options.

5. Choose whether to crop slides to fit landscape or portrait orientation.

6. Choose an option from the Preview Quality list. Your choices are High, Medium, and Low. The High option gives you the best image quality with the largest file size.

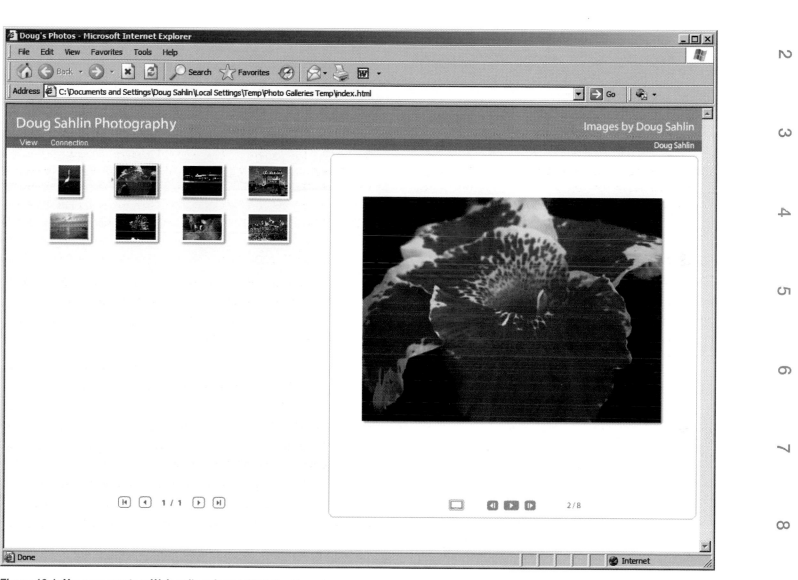

Figure 10-1: You can create a Web gallery from within the Organizer.

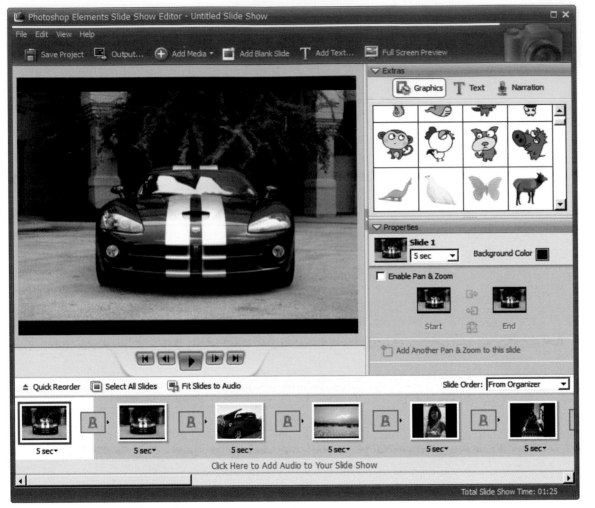

7. Click **OK** to open the Photoshop Elements Slide Show Editor. In the Editor, you can add extras to your slide show in the form of graphics, text, or narration. You can also modify the default background color and duration for each slide.

8. To add a pan and zoom to a slide, click the **Pan And Zoom** check box. When you do this, crop marks appear around the slide. You set the size of the slide at the start and end of the display duration, which determines how the slide is panned and zoomed. Note that some transitions will not work when you save a slide show as a PDF document.

9. Click the **Click Here To Add Audio** icon at the bottom of the workspace to navigate to a soundtrack on your computer, which will play during your slide show. If you add a soundtrack to the show, click **Fit Slides To Audio** to change the duration of the slide show to match the audio.

10. The icons at the top of the workspace enable you to save the project; choose how the slide show will be output; add photos, video, or audio to the show; add a blank slide to the show; add text to slides; and preview the slide show in Full Screen mode.

CREATING A CALENDAR

You can also use Photoshop Elements to create a custom calendar with your digital pictures. You can choose from many different layouts. You create the calendar by selecting 12 photos from the Organizer and then choosing **Create A Calendar** from the Create drop-down list. The calendar is printed by Kodak EasyShare Gallery. When you first choose to do this, you're prompted to create an account, after which you can order the calendar.

ORDERING PRINTS ONLINE

You can order prints online by dragging images from the Organizer to the Order Prints palette in the lower-right corner of the workspace. You can have the prints sent to a friend, colleague, or to yourself. You must be online to order prints. The printing is done by Adobe Photoshop Services, which is provided by Kodak EasyShare Gallery.

11. Click **Output** to display the Slide Show Output dialog box. The options differ, depending on the output you choose. Figure 10-2 shows the slide show that was output as a PDF slide show, which, by default, is displayed in Full Screen mode.

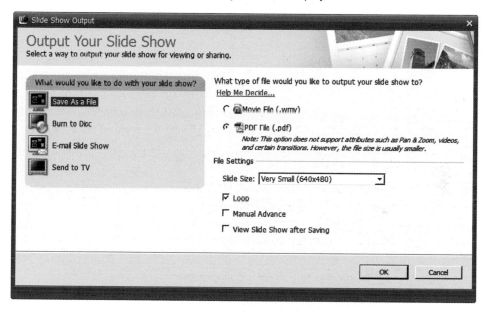

Figure 10-2: You can create custom slide shows from your photos.

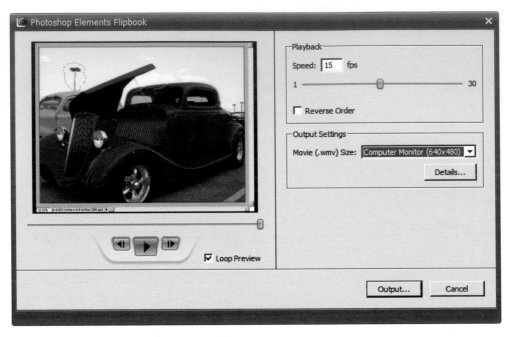

Create a Flip Book

Another way you can display your images is by creating a flip book. You can create a flip book for computer viewing, for playback on a DVD player, for display on a Web site, for sharing via e-mail, or for output as a video compact disc (VCD) for viewing on a DVD player that can read VCDs. To create a flip book:

1. Choose the images for your flipbook from the Organizer.

2. Choose **Flip Book** from the Create drop-down list to display the Photoshop Elements Flip Book dialog box.

3. Specify the speed of your slide show. The default option of 15 fps (frames per second) is good for computer viewing. Specify a speed of 30 fps if you're outputting the flipbook as a DVD or VCD. You can manually enter a value in the text box, or drag the slider to specify the speed.

4. Choose an option from the Movie Size drop-down list. Your options are:

   ● **DVD-NTSC (720 × 480)** is suited for playback on DVD players in North and South America.

   ● **DVD-PAL (720 × 576)** is suited for playback on a European DVD player.

   ● **Computer Monitor (640 × 480)** is suited for playback on a computer.

   ● **Web (320 × 240)** is suitable for playback on a Web site.

   ● **E-mail (160 × 120)** is suited for e-mail distribution.

   ● **VCD-NTSC (352 × 240)** is suited for playback on DVD players that can play VCD disks in North and South America.

   ● **VCD-PAL (352 × 288)** is suited for playback on a European DVD player that can read VCD disks.

NOTE

The quality of a VCD slide show is similar to the quality of a video on a good VHS tape.

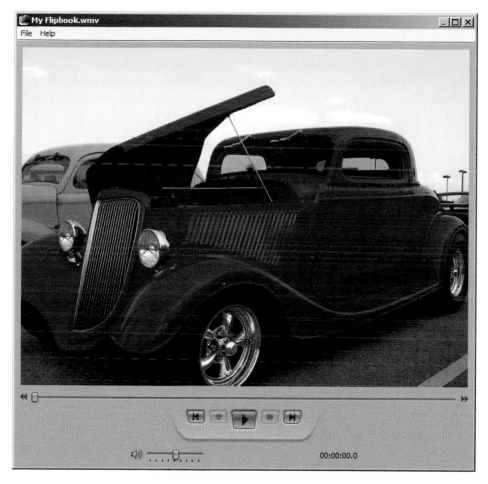

5. Click **Output** to open the Save As WMV (Windows Media Video) dialog box.

6. Enter a name for the flipbook, and then click **Save**. The illustration shows a completed flipbook for monitor viewing.

Print Your Digital Photos

It's wonderful to edit your digital photos in Photoshop Elements and share them electronically with friends via e-mail and your Web site. However, nothing quite matches the thrill of being able to look at a printed image that is suitable for framing. If you own a photo-quality printer, as discussed in Chapter 1, you can print hard copies of your digital pictures. In the sections that follow, you'll learn how to print your images from Photoshop Elements, and choose the right paper.

Print Your Photos After Previewing Them

There's an old saying that what you see is what you get. The Photoshop Elements design team gives credence to this wisdom, as they've included a Print command with a dialog box that enables you to preview the end result. When you use the Print command, you can resize and reposition the photo relative to the media on which you are printing the image.

1. In the Full Edit or Quick Fix workspace, open the image you want to print.

2. Choose **File | Print** to open the Print Preview dialog box, as shown in the following illustration.

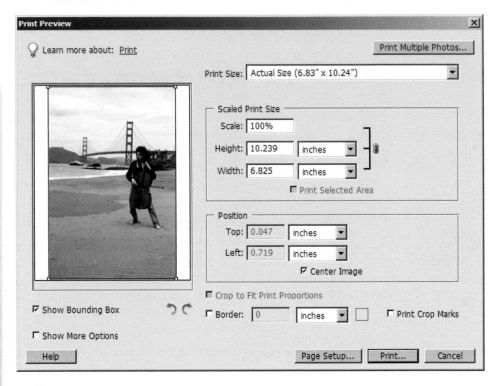

3. Click the **Page Setup** button to select the paper size, source, and orientation.

4. Select an option from the Print Size drop-down list.

5. Clear the **Center Image** check box if you want to manually position the image within the media. After doing this, you can type values for the top and left position of the image, or click inside the image and drag it to the desired position. This option is handy if the image is smaller than the selected paper size.

6. Drag a corner handle to resize the image within the media. Alternatively, you can type a value in the Width or Height field to resize the image proportionately.

7. Click the **Show More Options** check box to reveal options for color management and for displaying a caption and/or file name on the printed image.

8. To rotate the image, click the **Rotate 90 Degrees Left** or **Rotate 90 Degrees Right** icon.

9. Click the **Border** check box to add a border to the image. If you choose this option, enter a value in the Border text field, and then click the Color Picker to specify a color for the border.

10. Click the **Corner Crop Marks** check box to add crop marks around the image. This option creates useful guides that can be used to cut the photo to size with a paper trimmer.

11. Click **Print** to print the image.

Index